Rendezvous Country

IMAGES OF AMERICA SERIES

AMERICAN WEST PUBLISHING COMPANY
PALO ALTO, CALIFORNIA

Rendezvous Country

Photographs by David Muench • Text by Donald G. Pike

Gannett Peak in the Wind River Range of Wyoming.

OVERLEAF: *The Teton Range in the white quiet of winter.*

Library of Congress Cataloging in Publication Data

Muench, David.
    Rendezvous country.

    (Images of America series)
    Includes index.
    1. Photography—Landscapes. 2. The West—De-
scription and travel—Views. 3. Fur trade—the
West. I. Pike, Donald G. II. Title.
TR660.5.M83   779'.9'9780924   75-6323
ISBN 0-910118-65-5
ISBN 0-910118-66-3 de luxe

FIRST EDITION

Contents

PAGES 6–7: *In a world built on rock, life grips the highest alpine reaches of the Wind River Range with a shallow foothold.*

PAGES 8–9: *Sunrise tints peaks of the Cathedral Group in the Tetons above Jackson Hole.*

In splendid isolation, the Dinwoody River snakes down the narrow domain it has carved for itself in the Wind River Range.

The long, soft light of autumn warms faded memories of traplines along the banks of the Stillwater Fork of Bear River in Utah.

Etched by the elements and aproned with snow, Granite Peak in the Beartooth Range scribes
a rugged northern boundary on rendezvous country.

Through the park that now bears its name, Yellowstone River flows in an
arresting counterpoint of virgin water and much-labored rock.

The Wild Land

It stands at the center of the north-south sweep of the Rocky Mountains, just astraddle the continental divide on the east, rolling and rising to the western edge of the cordillera. It is a land of high mountains capped with eternal snows, and poorly nourished alpine slopes that spread down through dense pine forests dotted with verdant oases of meadow and aspen, to broad foothills of scrub oak and mountain mahogany. It is also a land of small, fertile river valleys standing knee-deep in natural hay, and broad, arid basins that stretch for thousands of square miles in an undulating desert of sagebrush and short grass. It is a region that finds no unity in a similarity of geography, climate, vegetation, or river systems. It pays no homage to the artificial political boundaries of man, gathering its estate from the Rocky Mountains of western Wyoming and eastern Idaho, and reaching to the south to grasp the northeast corner of Utah. It is rendezvous country, finding its unity in the minds and actions of men, bound together in a mood and character that celebrate its past.

In the morning mist that rises from a beaver pond with the first blush of a fall sunrise, rendezvous country evokes the presence of other men and another time. They were men who came to the region in search of furs and found not only a living but a way of life, in a wilderness that taxed their strength, courage, and skill in the most elemental coin possible—survival. They ate from the land, were sheltered and clothed by it, and were accorded the kind of freedom that only wilderness can offer to men who would be their own law. In return the mountain men accepted the land for what it was, taking from it only as another predator, never seeking to make of the land anything the land had not made of itself.

Rendezvous country is a region that has retained its character despite the presence of modern man. It continues to be a land so suited to the life and ethics of another era that the ghosts of the white men who first coursed its streams and rivers still stalk the memories and imaginations of the people who call it home today. The

Fog filters softly through Rock Creek Basin in the Beartooths—high country where both man and beast find survival a tenuous proposition.

way of the mountain man is yet firmly a part of this region, for most of it remains the province of nature. It is wild land, where man doesn't call the shots but must accommodate himself to a world bigger and stronger than himself.

Towns have risen, even small cities, and ranchers, farmers, and loggers have cut inroads into every part of it, but they all do so with the firm knowledge that they are not undisputed masters of the situation. Any who lack this knowledge run the risk of meeting an abrupt death, or such severe frustration that they depart cursing, not their own lack of perception and skill, but some intangible called bad luck. And they are diminished by their exile, for they not only miss the beauty and drama of this land, but they have failed to learn to measure themselves. They have failed to experience the fulfillment of one who finds in himself the skill and discretion to live with and use the land, as neither master nor slave.

The parameters of rendezvous country were laid by the men who came to trade annually at Rocky Mountain fairs. The first, in 1825, was held on Henrys Fork of the Green River; in 1826 and 1831, in Cache Valley, where Bear River makes its great turn around the Wasatch; in 1827 and 1828, on the broad meadows around Bear Lake (on the Utah-Idaho line); in 1829 and 1838, in the valley of the Popo Agie (with a later, ancillary meeting at Pierre's Hole); in 1830, near the confluence of the Wind River and the Bighorn (or, more precisely, where geographers changed the name of the Wind to Bighorn—the Indians and mountain men knew it was the same river); in 1832, at Pierre's Hole; in 1834, on Hams Fork of Green River; and in 1833, 1835–37, and 1839–40, along the banks of Green River itself, usually in the vicinity of Horse Creek or New Fork.

Although the quest for pelts might take a trapper south to the Sangre de Cristo Range in modern New Mexico, or north beyond the Missouri River, or as far west as California and Oregon, the summer always brought a return to this ring of mountains and the basin they encircled. From the north, and pointing southeast along the continental divide, the Wind River Range provides the highest and most rugged arm of the circle. Its eastern flank is traced by the Wind River and its valley down to a confluence with the Popo Agie near where the parallel mountains disappear beneath the plains. South from the end of the Wind Rivers, stretching away in the wide and rolling country that became the gateway for a nation moving west, is South Pass and the broken hill country that drops off to the west of the continental divide. Spanning the southern reaches of rendezvous country are the Uinta Mountains, which break tradition with the rest of the Rockies by lying emphatically east and west. To the west lies the northern end of the Wasatch Range, outlined by the incredible course of Bear River, which runs north off the skirts of the Uintas for nearly a hundred miles, before bending in a great westerly arc around the Wasatch and heading due south for Great Salt Lake. The northwestern corner of rendezvous country is completed in the interlocking chain of the Salt River, Snake River, and Teton ranges.

It is, as one student of the region remarked, "a geographer's nightmare," for it responds to no simple generalizations. The waters of three great river systems are spawned here—the Missouri (in Wind River), the Colorado (in the Green), and the Columbia (in the Snake River headwaters)—in what seems to be an interlocking network of tributaries. Consider the case of the Green and the Bear: tributaries of Blacks Fork, which in turn joins the Green, rise within ten miles of the upper reaches of the Bear, and yet the Green and the Bear parallel one another, flowing in opposite directions into entirely different bodies of water seven hundred miles apart. It was enough to ruin a mountain man's whole day, especially if he was a little lost in the first place.

Along the western slope of the Wind River Range, in the land where the river of the Seedskeedee is born, Table Mountain is reflected in a Green River lake.

The heart of rendezvous country is the Green River Basin, which is enfolded by these mountains, a broad depression that varies from amply watered ranch- and farmland along its western and northern reaches to semiarid saltbush and greasewood desert in the southeast. The basin lies in the rain shadow of the surrounding mountains, where water-laden clouds riding the prevailing westerlies are forced high to precipitate their moisture, leaving little for the basin. The rivers born in the runoff from the mountains therefore become essential to survival in the basin, and life congregates along their courses.

The major artery of the basin is the Green River, which begins life high on the slopes of the Wind River Range and is fed during the course of its journey by hundreds of creeks and streams that rise in the Snake River, Salt River, and Uinta mountains. The Indians had named the river Seedskeedee (or Seat Kadee, Siskadee, or Seetskeedee—take your pick as they are all just a marginally literate white man's rendering of an Indian word) in honor of the prairie chicken who annually puffs up his throat, ruffles his feathers, and dances a thundering mating ritual along its banks. The mountain men retained the name until government mapmakers decided about 1840 that the Spaniards who called it Rio Verde knew more about the river than the trappers, and changed the name to Green River. Bernard DeVoto staunchly maintained that it was really the Colorado River, which it joins in southern Utah, because it is not only longer than the fork now known as the

Colorado River, but it shows more characteristics in common with the lower portion of the Colorado. Fortunately, there are enough long-time residents who still insist that the Indians were right and, the professional meddlers be damned, that the river and the basin it drains will always be known as the Seedskeedee.

Rendezvous country as we know it today first started to take shape in the fire and folding of the Laramide revolution that began to lift the entire Rocky Mountain chain a hundred million years ago. In a series of pulses and pauses the upheaval continued for almost fifty million years, as great granite cores pushed up to form mountains like the Wind Rivers. The land shattered along fault lines, huge blocks tilted up to form abrupt scarps like the western face of the Wasatch, and the pressure of the earth's displaced skin squeezed and folded basins into ranges. Wind and water began their slow but inexorable work, gradually eroding the new land, cutting declivities and canyons, wearing and weathering the mountains to the wrinkled respectability of age.

About three million years ago the wind and water were joined by Pleistocene glaciers, which moved forward at least three times to mold and scrape the region, serrating ridges and carving huge U-shaped valleys. As they retreated, the glaciers left terminal moraines—the great prows of rock and rubble the ice pushed ahead of itself—to block small canyons and create the myriad lakes that remain today on the slopes. By most reckonings the Ice Age is past, but high in sun-sheltered clefts of the Wind River Range a number of small glaciers survive, waiting for the world's temperature to drop a few degrees so they can complete the work they started.

Weather is the final arbiter of life in rendezvous country, and it exercises this prerogative in an infinite number of moods of wind, rain, heat, snow, and cold. It determines what will blossom, and what must suffer the slow death of drought; it brings gentle zephyrs and warm rains that nurture and encourage life, but it also can lay fierce winds and long, cold winters on the land, gripping plants and animals in a fist that is as ruthless as drought. But while weather may strike extremes or change with dizzying abruptness, it sustains life because every plant and creature has accepted these facts and adapted itself accordingly—and life is very good for those that have found their place.

The land of the Seedskeedee rises in the path of the prevailing westerly winds that blow across the continent all year. Although these winds carry most of the moisture that collects here, the mountains are the agent of delivery, forcing the clouds up into cooler air where they precipitate rain and snow. Thus the mountains will register rainfall of twenty or more inches per year, while the valleys and basin on the eastern lee of the mountains are lucky to gather eight or ten inches.

Wind is a fact of life in the region. During the winter it blows hard and dry across the basin, churning equally dry and gritty snow into blinding ground blizzards and giving rise to the kind of local wit that suggests that not much snow falls, but a lot blows through; and that what does fall, doesn't melt—it just blows around until it wears out. Winds are also created within the region, bringing the sudden changes in local climate that surprise newcomers. As the first rays of the morning sun warm the air high in mountain valleys, the air rises, drawing cool breezes from the lower, moister valleys. By afternoon this cool, damp air will have been pushed against the mountain heights, precipitating a sudden, brief thundershower. There is probably no more dramatic wind that blows through rendezvous country, however, than the fabled chinook.

The warm, dry winds of the chinook strike suddenly in the winter and spring, sometimes raising the temperature forty degrees in a half-

Twilight begins to work its subtle magic with the land and water of the lower Green River Lakes, along the apron of the Wind River Range.

hour and thawing the snowpack into an avalanche of floodwaters. The chinook is born in cold, wet winds that rise up the western slope of the mountains, cooling still more until all the moisture is wrung out as rain or snow. The condensation necessary for precipitation raises the temperature of the air, and as the wind starts down the eastward slope it is warmed by the decreasing altitude, until it arrives in the basin as a dry, warm wind.

The mountains and their weather combine to lay a varied mantle of plant life over the region in a patchwork of grasses, flowers, bushes, and trees that succor man and wildlife alike. But while the variety may seem infinite, there is an orderly system of life zones at work. In the semi-arid lowland of the basin, sagebrush, saltbrush, hop sage, and greasewood predominate, their hard-surfaced exteriors and sparse foliage resisting desiccation by wind and sun. The short grasses that grow here—needle grass and buffalo grass—are similarly narrow stemmed and deep rooted, gathering all the water available and relinquishing as little as possible. But in the well-watered river bottoms that cut across the basin, broad-leaved trees like cottonwood, box elder, and willow can thrive.

As the land begins to rise, as at the eastern end of the Uintas, the sagebrush gives way (if rainfall is adequate) to grasslands of blue grama and bluestem, which are laced with lupine and other wild flowers in the spring. Higher still is foothill scrub, where the grasses are joined by low-growing mountain mahogany and juniper. At about 6,000 feet the montane, or timbered mountain, zone begins, rising through growths of yellow pine, Douglas fir, lodgepole pine, and, as the altitude approaches 10,000 or 11,000 feet, stands of Engelmann spruce, whitebark pine, and subalpine fir. At almost any point from foothills to timberline where creeks and springs create lush meadows, quaking aspen and willow take over in a glittering exuberance of sunlight and color. Above timberline, in the rocky, wind-swept country of long winters, sedges, bear grass, and tiny alpine flowers burst in a brief frenzy of growth before the early snows protect them from high arctic winds.

Latitude changes the relative altitudes of zones; to the north, in the Wind River Range, for instance, timberline begins at about 10,000 feet, while farther south, in the Uintas, the greater exposure to sunlight and marginally lower temperatures raises timberline to 11,000 feet. But probably a greater disparity is noted in the microclimates created by a slope's exposure to the sun. In a typical mountain river valley, the slopes to the north—which face south and consequently the sun for more hours during the day—will be thick with conifers and aspen, while the more shaded slopes to the south will support mountain mahogany and scrub oak. The valley at the same time will maintain box elder and cottonwood, interspersed with aspen, meadow grass, and garlands of wild flowers.

It is this interweaving of life zones, rather than any orderly pattern, that typifies the whole of rendezvous country. It is a land that defies generalization or simple consistency in a triumphant insistence on pursuing life in its own way. And in this the land was characteristic of the men who first found a living, and then a lifeway, in it—and in some measure those who still do today.

22

Home of the Beaver

There is a story told—usually in the warmth of the winter lodge when the cold outside lies like a thin, white blanket on the long sleep of the land—of a time before man had set his foot in this world. It is a story best told after children have been sated out of restiveness by full stomachs and the bundled warmth of buffalo robes, when old men can hunker close by a fire to soothe the quiet pain that squeezes deep in aging joints, while the wind tugs futilely at the skirts of the tipi. Time slows, stops, then reels backward as the old men unlimber their memories on the days when the rains fell until a great flood covered everything, and there was no place left to stand. It was Beaver, the wisest of all the creatures, who was called upon to make a world again for all the other live things. Beaver dove deep below the water, scooping up sticks and mud with his forepaws to make a great mound, much as he does today when building his lodge. He worked long and hard, never ceasing his labors until the job was done, and there was a dry-land part of the world again with plains, forests, and mountains for all the other animals.

Of all the creatures who make their home in rendezvous country, only the beaver could have done it, and the children could see the truth of the old men's tale along almost any stream or river they passed. The beaver created a world of his own wherever he decided to settle, and he did it with a wisdom and dedicated effort that transcended the expectations even of old men and small children. Other animals might burrow out a den or warren, and some might even store a bit of food for the winter, but only the beaver was dissatisfied enough with the world as he found it to make his own pond by building a dam, to construct a home that was virtually impervious to assault, and to store his food where only he could get to it. Wherever he went, the beaver created a micro-world suited to himself, although most of the other creatures, too, found it to be—at one time or another—a very fine place indeed.

The beaver is the second largest rodent in the

world, but in keeping with an industrious character, he never stops trying: from the time of his birth until the moment of death, the beaver is continually growing. In the course of a life that normally spans about twelve years, a healthy specimen will reach four feet long and tip the scales between forty and sixty pounds, although there are a few instances of beavers weighing as much as a hundred pounds. The wide, flat tail, which contributes twelve to sixteen inches to the total length, is thick and scaly—a feature which won the beaver special dispensation as a fish during the eighteenth century, in order that his flesh might be eaten on days of fasting. The tail serves as a rudder and diving plane while swimming and provides the third leg on the stool when a beaver sits upright to fell a tree; its resounding slap on the water is the universal alarm system (a reflex so conditioned that beaver on land will flail the earth when threatened).

Directly descended from the giant Castorides, a 700-pound beaver that stalked the wetlands of the world a million years ago, the beaver has evolved into a magnificently adapted aquatic mammal. He swims with large, webbed hind feet, stroking in unison while cruising but switching to a furious alternating paddle for high speed. Underwater a transparent eyelid closes, allowing clear vision while protecting the sensitive eye from debris and grit. The mouth is similarly adapted, with flaps of flesh that close behind the teeth, permitting the beaver to gnaw or bite and hold while submerged without collecting a mouthful of water in the process. Beavers normally remain underwater from three to five minutes, although most can manage eight minutes when necessary, a circumstance made possible by extremely efficient lungs (a beaver utilizes 75% of potential capacity, man about 20%), which have a high tolerance for accumulated carbon dioxide. Probably most amazing, though, is the metabolic change that occurs when diving: the heart slows, and the blood vessels to the legs constrict, forcing more blood to the brain and other vital organs.

If the beaver has a fatal flaw, it lies in his mechanism for keeping warm. As the temperature drops with the onset of winter and the water approaches 32 degrees, the outer hairs of his pelt begin to lengthen and the soft underfur grows thick and dense. This luxurious fur is microscopically barbed, and it was this fact that brought the white man to haunt the home of the beaver with steel traps. During the early eighteenth century, fashionable hats were made by felting, a process that involved little more than dampening fur and pressing it firmly together. Unfortunately for the beaver, his winter coat with its tiny barbs had superior matting and clinging properties. But Brer Beaver was a pretty crafty critter, and that helped to put a little extra distance between him and the hat racks of London.

The beaver's cycle of life begins under the ice-locked ponds in January or February, when the mating urge signals that the time for perpetuating his own kind has come. Beavers are normally monogamous for life, with little fighting for mates and few harems; there are often a number of aging, widowered bachelor beavers. Even in large colonies the nuclear family, living together in its own lodge, is the normal social unit.

In the winter lodge a breeding pair will oversee the activities of young that are nearly two years old, as well as last year's kits; but as the ice clears in the spring, the female, who feels her time coming on, will drive the two-year-olds from the lodge and the pond. The bewildered vagrants, abruptly cast out to find a new home, have been the victims of a mother's understanding—her understanding that the food resources of the pond are finite, and that, if her home is to be sustained, somebody has to leave. A two-year-old's lot is not particularly grim, however, for he has had considerable education.

Just before giving birth in May, the female will exercise her ire once more, chasing the male and kits out of the lodge to find temporary residence in abandoned lodges or holes in the bank. Once alone, the female will bear from four to six kits weighing about a pound apiece; often the deliveries are spread over as long as three days. The young are born well developed, amply furred, and with eyes wide open—they will be swimming in less than a day with no instruction. The male and yearlings are usually permitted to return shortly thereafter.

Spring and summer are a time of indolence and relaxation for the beaver, a release from the close quarters and drab diet of winter. Young and old alike spurn willows and bark altogether, apparently having had their fill during the winter; they concentrate instead on the new shoots of grass, early skunk cabbage, ferns, and succulent bulbs rooted out of the ground. Everything green and juicy is fair fodder for these voracious herbivores; they will drift in the water feeding on lilies, rushes, and any other aquatic plant life, or venture into the tall meadow grasses for columbine, thistleroot, Indian paintbrush, and fruit in season. Where available, beavers will snack on mushrooms and the brilliant snowflower.

Before the arrival of man beavers were diurnal, working by day and sleeping at night. But increased hunting pressure forced a change, and now they prefer to emerge near dusk, spending the daylight hours within the sanctuary of the lodge. Even so, the lure of the sun occasionally proves too strong, and a beaver will stretch out on his roof or dam to bask in the warmth and groom his coat. The beaver grooms with a split claw located on the inside of each hind foot, drawing the fine-tooth comb through the fur, removing small parasites, tangled hair, and accumulated grit. The pelt clean, he will dab at the castor glands just under his tail and spread the pungent liquid through the fur, returning the slick oils lost during his time in the water. It is a relaxing but necessary pastime, for a waterlogged beaver has all the aquatic potential of an anchor.

The soothing, well-fed months of summer can easily become narcotic, lulling the beaver into a relaxed sense of security; but while the living is easy, this is also the time of maximum danger. From now until winter closes in, the beaver will be ranging far from the safety of his lodge, cruising the shoreline and moving across dry ground, where his waterborne grace turns to a slow and awkward waddle. Unless he is extremely cautious and alert, a beaver on land will easily fall victim to the predatory coyotes, wolves, mountain lions, bobcats, wolverines, and bears that gather in the web of nature that surrounds the beaver's world.

Probably the most wide-ranging and adaptable of the animals that periodically appear to prey near the beaver's pond is the coyote, the wily canine who figures as a symbol on the skyline in every sagebrush saga of the West. He pursues his livelihood from the arid desert lowlands to the barren scarps above timberline, succeeding because he is cautious, cunning, and willing to feed on anything that is available. Coyotes are primarily carnivorous, caring little whether they catch and kill a meal themselves, or dine on the carrion left by others. But when times are hard and the stomach pinches, they will eat bugs, insects, and roughage—and even seem to seek out an occasional berry patch.

Often maligned as a mangy, skulking varmint, the coyote is really quite a delicate dog, smaller than a collie and more fleet and graceful than most of his canine relations. His color will range from shades of gray, through tan, to dark brown, and during a severe winter the dark-tipped coat will bloom into a luxurious pelt.

Coyotes normally mate for life, raising a litter of a half-dozen pups through the spring and summer of each year. The female prefers hollow logs, rock crevices, caves, or dens cut in arroyo banks, for raising the young through the first two months until they are weaned. Even after the pups begin their outdoor education, they will return daily to the den to rest. They are taught to hunt tiny meadow mice and ground squirrels, as well as the larger rock chucks and jackrabbits. They learn that cunning is more important than speed in catching sage grouse, that delicacy outweighs brute strength when making a meal of a porcupine, and that teamwork is necessary to run down even an ailing pronghorn. They soon find out, too, that they are no match for healthy deer, elk, or moose, so they must concentrate on the weak and sick—a circumstance helpful to every species.

The pups depart in the fall, nearly grown, to seek out less crowded territory for themselves. During the winter many will starve or be crushed under the hooves of a miscalculation, but the smartest and the quickest will survive, improving other species and cleaning up the garbage, plotting and adapting all the while.

Less numerous, less visible, less adaptable, and more misunderstood is the coyote's larger relative, the wolf. Once very numerous in rendezvous country, the wolf today is a rarity, forced back by a bad reputation for stock killing—rarely deserved—and a natural reluctance for any contact with man. Wolves are efficient hunters, capable of dragging down even elk and moose, but this usually occurs during the winter when small packs follow the migrating herds, pulling down the weakest animals in a group effort. Random renegades do appear who prefer calves and lambs—an appetite that brings the wrath of man on all predators—but normally wolves prefer the solitude of wilderness, feeding on rodents and culling the unfit.

Like coyotes, wolves mate for life, often keeping several generations of pups together in the pack. They are also gregarious, usually accepting lonesome outsiders into the group to share in the hunting and pup-raising chores; often several "families" will amiably coexist in a sort of large, extended clan. But what they have staked out as their territory is inviolate, and packs that trespass have to fight or run.

Wolves maintain a large hunting range, often several hundred square miles, and therefore con- stitute no real threat to the continued existence of any species. In spite of all the hysteria and flaming adjectives that the mere mention of wolves invariably precipitates, it is comforting to remember that *they* have never hunted, or farmed, or urban-sprawled another species completely into oblivion.

Another shy victim of man's encroachment is the mountain lion. Whether known as cougar, puma, panther, painter, or catamount, he is a retiring creature who avoids contact with man at almost all cost. This tawny cat, lighter on the throat and underside, is a wraithlike presence in the wild—silent, cautious, and a consummate still hunter. The staple of the mountain lion's diet is deer, although failing venison, the cat will feed on anything from moose to field mice— even extending the chase into shallow water after beavers, muskrats, or ducks and geese.

The traditional image of a mountain lion, hunkered on an overhanging limb or rock waiting for an unsuspecting doe to wander by, is accurate as far as it goes. Just as often, however, the big cat will stalk silently to within a few jumps of its prey before striking to break the back or crush the skull. The attack must be short and abrupt, for the lion is far too slow to catch a deer that has reached a terrified top speed. A healthy adult will consume about eight pounds of meat after a kill and then cover the carcass by scratching up a mound of leaves, dirt, and branches before leaving. Never wasteful—or perhaps just lazy—the lion will return time and again to feed on the rapidly ripening meat until it is all eaten.

Mountain lions meet, breed, and separate in a brief and often furious mating session. For only a few weeks every two or three years the female will tolerate a male companion, who must fight deadly encounters with other toms for the privilege. After the female is bred, the male returns to his solitary life; if he approaches when the kittens are in the den, the female will likely kill him—which is only fair, since he would eat the young if she weren't there. The kittens, usually two or three, are supervised and taught by the female, usually until the fall of their second year.

If the critters of rendezvous country gave a medal to the animal who most bedeviled mankind, it would surely go to the wolverine—although by now there are so few left in the old beaver country that it might have to be given posthumously. Mountain men seldom admitted, though, that the wolverine was mere animal; a trapper in his cups at rendezvous might be "half-man, half-alligator," but a wolverine was half-bear, half-devil.

This bent, misshapen creature with the awkward lope, long, powerful forelegs, and wickedly curving claws is really a large weasel, weighing thirty-five to forty pounds. His reputation for mayhem and destruction, however, belies his size and demeanor. He is a formidable opponent for any other animal, fighting with a fury and tenacity matched only by the badger; he has, as a matter of record, chased cougars, wolves, and black bears off their dinners. His real specialty, though, seems to be making life miserable for man. The wolverine will trail a trapline, stealing the bait, devouring the trapped animals, and even hiding the traps—all without ever being caught himself. He will break into a cabin, eat all the food, then literally demolish everything inside; at times he has even been known to take a stab at tearing down the walls.

The wolverine will eat anything he can take from someone else, as well as any rodents, crippled or ill big game, birds, fish, or berries that he can find himself. Killing is done with little grace or speed, usually by slashing with the claws or biting at the spine. He is so clumsy and so voracious that he will eat a porcupine whole—often resulting in his untimely death.

It may be that the wolverine is as ornery as he seems, for he shuns even the company of his own kind when possible. Mating is a brief en-counter in the spring; three or four young are whelped in July and sent out to fend for themselves in the fall when only two-thirds grown. Presumably a mother's love does have limits.

Despite the wolverine's considerable reputation for violence and destruction, he is no match for either of the great bears when they go on the prod. A great deal is made of the difference between black and grizzly bears, but in their habits and predilections they are quite similar. Both bears are omnivorous (though the grizzly is classified as a carnivore), and both will eat carrion as well as anything else animal or vegetable they can find. Even the smaller blacks are awesomely powerful, though not very capable hunters. They are generally conceded to be slightly more even tempered than grizzlies, concentrating on herbage in their diet, but they will eat rodents and can sometimes even pull down a young deer or elk.

Both species are solitary creatures, enjoying the company of other bears only during the brief spring mating season. They do not hibernate but simply go into a deep sleep, during which respiration slows slightly but body temperature remains the same. The female awakes in January to give birth to one or more toothless and almost hairless cubs, which she nurses inside the den until spring, when they emerge as fully equipped, if tiny, replicas of their mother.

The biggest difference between the grizzly and black lies in the number still extant. The once numerous grizzlies were hunted and trapped almost out of existence because occasionally one bear would turn to stock killing. The great dish-faced, humpbacked grizzly is capable of killing any other animal in rendezvous country, but because he prefers the barren land above timberline, much of the meat in his diet is comprised of rock chucks and burrowing rodents, which he digs out in a roaring cacophony of flying dirt and cascading rocks. He often ranges down into the river bottoms, though most animals that share his range have learned to give him wide berth.

Along the northern fringe of rendezvous country, in the Absaroka Range, the undisturbed solitude of Brooks Lake captures eons of geologic evolution for a quiet instant.

Of all the predators in rendezvous country, the beaver's greatest natural enemy is undoubtedly the otter. This is not because otters have a voracious appetite for beavers or because they are viciously efficient killers. It is due rather to the fact that when an otter decides on a beaver kit meal, there is no escape. The otter is a better, faster swimmer than the beaver, and the lodge that offers the beaver protection from every other predator, becomes a death trap. It is a rare otter, however, that will fight a furiously protective mother beaver just for a meal, especially since the pond usually offers fish, crawdads, frogs, snakes, and salamanders in abundance.

Otters are the tumbling, glissading, hyperactive children of rendezvous country. They will play for hours, sliding on a muddy bank or complicating their hunting so that there is more chase and less catch. Because they are incessantly on the move, home may be fifty miles of mountain stream. But a pair will den up in a riverbank cave or abandoned beaver lodge for birthing, as the pups are completely helpless for nearly six weeks. Oddly enough, considering their eventual expertise, young otters have to be taught to swim—even encouraged to enter the water.

Among all the predators who come at some time to work the fringe of the world the beaver creates—and even to sample the creator—few enjoy it with the unmitigated glee of the otter. Here is a refuge from the other predators who would feed on him, filled with plenty of the best kinds of food, with all the work done by someone else. Even a wolverine might be satisfied with that.

As the days begin to shorten late in the summer, the beaver's pace quickens to complete preparations for the icebound months of winter. The lodge must be sealed above waterline, where the spring and summer rains have dissolved and washed away the mud veneer. The beaver gathers mud, tiny twigs, and dead grasses from the bottom of his pond, and clutching them to his chest with almost handlike front paws, staggers onto the lodge roof and dumps the load, patting it into place. In a seemingly endless round of scoops and dumps, he gradually builds a thick layer, leaving only a small vent open in the top.

The beaver must also stock his larder below the waterline. Through the winter he will feed on bark, so he gathers willow, aspen, and alder branches, spearing them into the muddy bottom of the pond near the lodge, weighting them with rocks if necessary. Trees with the sap flowing too freely are girdled and allowed to cure for a week on the bank before storage, as green bark will sour underwater. By the time the task is complete, a tangled mound of branches larger than the lodge will have grown up above the water.

The two-year-olds deported from the pond face a bigger task. They must build a dam and lodge as well as gathering the necessary food. Occasionally they will find a large existing pond that will tolerate new arrivals, or a dry hollow under a stream bank on a river too big and fast to freeze entirely, where they will risk daily excursions onto the land in search of food. But the beaver who finds a likely location, with ample food and building material close at hand, sets about the job of constructing a new home with a methodical persistence.

The dam must come first, and despite the beaver's popular reputation as an ingenious engineer, it is his tenacity, more than his skill, that gets the job done. Beavers will often dam at a less than ideal spot, when only a few hundred feet away a much shorter and lower dam would inundate more ground. Once he has chosen his location, admirable or not, a beaver will anchor a few branches on the bottom, gradually accumulating a low wall. He will use logs, branches, twigs, and rocks for a framework, adding mud as a sealant where necessary. The process seems haphazard, but the end result is solid enough to support even a moose and usually ruptures only slightly under the onslaught of spring floods. The lodge follows much the same construction of logs and branches piled together, with the entrance and interior carved out to suit the resident.

The beaver brings the same persistent attitude to his logging and can clear all the usable timber within hauling distance of his pond in only a few years. In felling a tree, he makes two cuts a few inches apart, one above the other, and pulls the intervening chip free. The process continues around the trunk and is gradually worked deeper until the tree falls. The notion that beavers can fell trees in a chosen direction is false. Cut timber often falls toward or into the water because trees, in their endless groping for sunlight, develop more foliage toward the open, or pond, side. This added weight naturally pitches the tree in a direction that is incidentally advantageous to the beaver.

In making his pond the beaver destroys one world and creates another. The fast water of the stream disappears, the trout's gravel spawning beds are silted over, and the meadow mice and ground squirrels who burrowed and fed along the grassy banks are pushed back before the accumulating water. But in turn the beaver creates an island of activity in the wilderness, where the quantity and intensity of life is compressed and quickened. The muddy bottom of the pond proves ideal for a wide variety of microscopic aquatic life—nymphs that will rise to the surface and hatch into a day-long frenzy of mating before laying their eggs in the water and dying. Trout will gather to feed on the nymphs, mayflies, and myriad other insects that prosper on the still, warm waters. Mergansers en route north or south in their semiannual migration will stop over and, diving below the surface, pursue the trout in a twisting race.

Muskrats and minks will come to join the pond, the muskrat with the kind of easy amiability that often earns him a nest in the beaver's lodge through the winter; the mink with a penchant for wanton slaughter of fish, rodents, and young birds that earns him nothing but fear and hostility. Deer will find the meadow grasses inviting, but moose will be even more enraptured, feeding on the water grasses and plants while satisfying a passion for wading in the cooling muck. The beaver's plan for the world may alter the land and shift the balance, but it suits most of his fellow creatures and does irreparable harm to none.

Before the white man made the beaver even more cautious than he naturally is, these gregarious rodents were abundantly spread over rendezvous country wherever the water flowed, from timberline to the central lowlands in the basin of the Seedskeedee. At one time of the year or another, the other animals were also residents of the various life zones, especially the grazers—the imperial elk, the moose, and the deer—who follow the grassland to feed in sheltered lowlands during the winter and return upcountry as the forest meadows green in the spring. There are others, however, especially adapted to the extremes of the land that seldom range far from familiar ground.

Down in the basin, on gently rolling plains, the pronghorn maintains his home. He is like no other creature on earth, and he is admirably suited to this open land where distance loses all perspective in a uniformity of sagebrush and bunchgrass. Though pronghorns are called antelope, they are not antelope: they have horns (a hard sheath over a bone core), not antlers (bony appendages that are shed annually). The horn is forked, however, and the outer sheath is shed every year—a phenomenon unique among horned species.

The pronghorn lives where his best attributes —sharp senses and great speed—are most useful. His extraordinarily keen eyesight can detect unusual movement four or five miles away, so few predators can approach on the open plains without arousing his suspicion; if approached, he has ample room to use his sixty-mile-per-hour speed for escape. When alarmed, the pronghorn tenses, flashing the white hairs on his rump and exuding a musk, thus alerting the rest of the herd. He survives because native grasses, greasewood, juniper, and sage provide an adequate diet, and because his body readily adjusts to extremes of temperature from 130 degrees in the summer to a numbing 40 degrees in the winter.

At the opposite extreme, high above timberline in the rocky and treeless domain of the bighorn sheep, there is a similar need for specific adaptation. The bighorn, content to feed on the green shoots of a brief growing season and able to paw through winter snow for feed the rest of the year, can survive extreme cold for long periods with little effect. Sharp eyesight offers advance warning of enemies, and a surefootedness on rocky crags unmatched by any other animal insures escape. This unparalleled alpine ability is due to an unusual foot, which combines an outer rim of hard hoof, essential to clinging on tiny ledges, with a soft inner pad that provides a supple, tactile surface for gripping.

In rendezvous country there is a place and role for every creature. Some are born to it, some have to learn it, and others have to carve out a niche for themselves, but in the end it all strikes a balance. That balance means that some have to die and others have to kill, and neither experience is easy or pretty. It is a great organic machine, pulsing with the creation and destruction that mark the passage of life, a test for the understanding of man if he is to share a part without destroying the whole. And by a dying fire in the winter lodge, old men remembered and children dreamed; they understood.

31

Cycles of Life

The world of living things in rendezvous country, from windswept alpine peaks to broad semiarid brush lands, projects an image of almost infinite variety. But every creature, every plant, is subject to the turn of the seasons; rising and falling, emerging and retreating, reproducing and dying under the gradual but inexorable presence of the climate's annual metamorphosis.

Winter can reign in deafening rage or awesome silence, but in either condition there are few live things that can argue with its dictates. It settles over the land like a long coma, killing or forcing drowsy retrenchment upon plants and animals alike. It is the time of starvation: starving for food, and starving for warmth.

But winter is a fast-fading memory in the presence of spring, when the land vibrates in the throes of rebirth. It is a time for repairing and renewing, for dramatic rejuvenation and splendid color, before the long pull of growth and development that marks the summer.

In fall the pace of life quickens, and the urgency of preparation for winter pervades the land. Plants and trees experience one last spasm of brilliant activity that tints them with the hues of autumn before dormancy. Some critters scurry about in the search for a secure lair or food to store in it; many are bound in the frenzy of mating; others simply leave.

It is a world of order and expectation, but it is never totally predictable—living things in this land can never be sure of when or how, only of the change within the cycle.

A trickle of life through winter's quiet shroud in Jackson Hole.

Dwarfed by the land and alone in the forbidding quiet of the mountain winter, a solitary moose trots purposefully across a meadow.

34

*For some critters, winter is the time of the big sleep, but others, like the mule deer,
must forage—and walk the ragged edge of survival.*

Rivers that resist the freeze remain oases of flowing life, their banks dimpled with the footprints of predator and prey alike, while birds course in the steam-soaked air above.

Harbinger of spring: a parry primrose along the Popo Agie River.

When spring arrives in the mountains, thawing streams break out with abandon,
heralding the time of renewal in a thunderous chorus.

*With the waters swept clear of ice by the spring thaw, the fertile meadows
along the Yellowstone begin the first tentative pulses out of dormancy.*

*For Brother Beaver spring is a mixed blessing:
lots of fresh buds and succulent greens to eat,
but a large ration of dam repair before the pond is safe.*

Unraveling like delicately feathered caterpillars, willow catkins open to meet the spring.

A young moose wallows in the favored warm-weather stalking grounds—
up to the hock in cooling muck, and chin deep in marsh grass.

In the high country of the Bridger Wilderness, columbine twists to face the sun.

Delicate in appearance, dainty in size, and thrifty throughout their life cycle,
wild flowers on the exposed alpine plateaus are hardy and resilient.

Even muted by the gray light of a gathering storm, Indian paintbrush provides one of the most dazzling displays ever daubed from Nature's palette.

Beaver lodge in the Green River: it looks like a pile of sticks and mud because that's what it is—Brother Beaver hollows out his lodge later.

Hunkered warily along the banks of the Green, a descendant of the lowly rodent that opened the American mountain West suns himself.

47

Among the scores of living creatures who share the beaver's world, a frog finds a roost and home in the pond.

Reflections off the clear waters of the Big Sandy mottle and obscure the wraithlike passage of a native cutthroat trout.

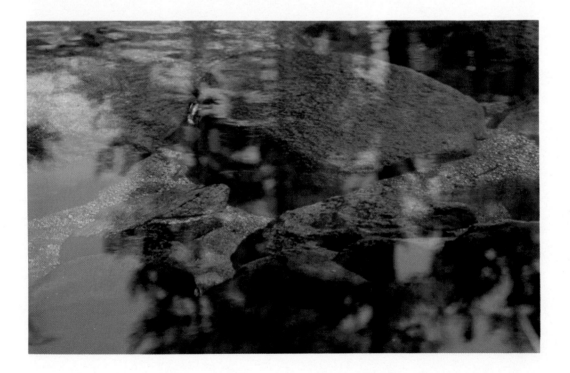

At the interface of land and pond, aquatic plants provide sustenance and shelter for creatures of both worlds.

A western horned owl, master predator upon the small rodents of meadow and field, surveys and assays the world with a swiveling, rapier-sharp gaze.

Nestled high in the Bridger Wilderness, a subalpine pool becomes a crossroads of mountain wildlife during the summer.

A gathering afternoon rain shower rushes up a valley towards culmination.
Boulders in the foreground were left by retreating glaciers.

High-country still life: natural bouquets of blue and white forget-me-not vie for attention on inhospitable ground.

Rising abruptly into a cobalt sky, Warbonnet Peak basks in its own reflected glory.

Once sprung from the earth and nurtured in its grace, now long dead, a victim of time and the elements, a gnarled ancient stands guard over new life—before returning to the earth forever.

Alert, agile, and altogether magnificent, bighorn sheep suffer man's presence poorly — and stand threatened by our intrusion into their world.

*Face of innocence, eyes of pride: they have known a life and seen
a world that could vanish in a footnote to our indifference.*

A sodbuster above timberline,
the pika cuts and cures his hay
in summer and stores it
for the long cold of winter.

Call him rock chuck, call him marmot,
call him "whistler," he is ever elusive,
a scrambling shadow among the rocks.

Unofficial symbol of a nation's westering, the buffalo had largely disappeared west of the divide before the Rocky Mountain fur trade had run its course.

Sunlight over the Beartooth country filters through a rydbergia.

*The midsummer felt still frosting his antlers, a healthy mule deer browses
in the deep valley grasses of the Popo Agie Primitive Area.*

OVERLEAF: *In the shifting half-light of a building storm, a young elk feeds along the Green River.*

Despite comic visage and ungainly appearance, a moose on the prod and bugling during the rutting season can become an agile, aggressive menace to the unwary.

Prints of the Moccasin

In the years soon after the first white men filtered into the country in search of rich beaver streams, a Mountain Crow Indian relaxing in his winter lodge on the flanks of the Wind River Range talked of his home:

The Crow country is exactly in the right place. It has snowy mountains and sunny plains; all kinds of climates and good things for every season. When the summer heats scorch the prairies, you can draw up under the mountains, where the air is sweet and cool, the grass fresh, and the bright streams come tumbling out of the snow-banks. There you can hunt the elk, the deer, the antelope, when their skins are fit for dressing; there you will find plenty of white bears and mountain sheep.

In the autumn, when your horses are fat and strong from the mountain pastures, you can go down into the plains and hunt the buffalo, or trap beaver on the streams. And when winter comes on, you can take shelter in the woody bottoms along the rivers; there

you will find buffalo meat for yourselves and cottonwood bark for your horses; or you may winter in the Wind River Valley, where there is salt weed in abundance.

The Crow country is exactly in the right place. Everything good is to be found there. There is no country like the Crow country.

He spoke as a Mountain Crow, recalling the blessings of the land of his people in the northern reaches of rendezvous country and letting the starving times and occasional brutal winter slip to forgotten recesses in his memory. He spoke as much of himself as he did of the land— a sense of his pleasure with the land and the life he found in it. He was satisfied with the world and the way it worked, so he must be in a very good place.

No one would have understood him better than the Shoshonis who ranged the land of the Seedskeedee south of the Wind Rivers. They lived at the heart of rendezvous country, from the Bear River to the Sweetwater, and south to the Uintas. The Shoshonis, too, had found their place, for life as it was meant to be lived was sustained, and the spiritual and temporal world continued to behave as their fathers said it should. They would have known that the old Crow was just fooling himself though, for they knew that it was really Shoshoni country that was exactly in the right place.

The deep love-of-place that both the Crows and the Shoshonis felt for their homeland was a natural, almost inevitable, outgrowth of their lifeway. This abiding affection developed because the Indian realized, and was content with the knowledge, that he was just another warm-blooded creature trying to find a place for himself in the world. He saw the land not for what it might be or could have been, but for what it was—and he accommodated himself to it. He found what the land had to offer in the way of food, clothing, shelter, and animal comforts, and adjusted his own needs and desires to fit what was available.

This adaptability, also translatable as an instinct for survival, bred a kind of easy contentment: if that is the way things are, then that is the way they ought to be. It was inconceivable for a man who daily measured his own frailty against the durability of the land and the power of the elements to harbor preconceptions about what the world should provide him, and thus the Indian was free of the frustrations attendant on men who would make the land over in their own image. Life was what the land offered, and if there was enough food to survive, then the Indian was content. It was neither a contrived philosophy nor a mindless acquiescence, but a way of life.

The Shoshonis, who held suzerainty over most of rendezvous country when the white man arrived, were the cultural heirs of hunters and gatherers who had ranged the basins and plains for twenty thousand years. Their ancestors were a people who had made a polished artistry of survival, hunting mammoth and great-horned bison on the plains and making do on rodents when big game was scarce; finding and rendering palatable every edible root and plant; drifting before droughts that turned waist-high grasslands into barren deserts; fashioning food, clothing, shelter, and weapons from whatever was available. It was a heritage of man as the prime predator, who overcame handicaps of slowness, small size, short fangs, and weak claws with cunning and an opposed thumb.

While the traditions of the Shoshonis ran deep, their roots were set in shallower soil. They were originally people of the Great Basin, who wandered into the land of the Seedskeedee about 1500. In the basin they had evolved patterns of living suited to survival in an essentially arid environment. Because food was usually available only in limited quantities, the bands were kept small to insure an adequate share for every member. Although not abundant, there was a broad base of plants and animals scattered around the basin, which kept the bands constantly on the move from one harvest to another. This continued mobility kept personal possessions and any kind of permanent shelter to a minimum. And the isolation afforded by the basin, protected from the depredation of high-plains raiders, kept the Shoshonis peaceable and more inclined to spend their time in the pursuit of food than warfare.

The movement into the mountain country, however, began to work subtle changes in the form and texture of Shoshoni life. Although the central basin of the Green River, with its limited rainfall and bunchgrass-and-sagebrush demeanor, may have often looked very much like home, the whole of the region provided a far richer and more varied world to the Shoshonis. Big game, especially bison and antelope, became an increasingly important staple of their diet, in addition to broadening and improving the source of raw materials for clothing and shelter. The

The name of the Snake River, intended to honor the Shoshonis who lived here, memorializes a trapper's misinterpretation of the sign-language symbol for the tribe.

myriad rivers and streams that tumbled out of the Uinta, Salt, and Wind River mountains laid green ribbons of cottonwood and dense foliage across the bottomlands, striping the basin with small-game refuges and tuber gardens. With the spring melt the high country was opened beyond timberline, yielding variety and abundance in the different life zones that wrapped the mountains from base to crest.

The Shoshonis had become a rich people in rendezvous country, but not simply because of the ready resources that relieved the endless scurry after sufficient food. They began to travel east of the divide onto the Plains, where they met, mingled, or fought with the Crows, Blackfeet, Kiowas, Comanches, and other Indians of the Plains tradition. It was a cultural commerce that introduced the Shoshonis to the tipi, better weapons, and a society dominated by the warrior ethic. The Shoshonis were learning a new way to live in their new land, and now an even bigger change—thanks to unseen, unsuspected men with pale features—was wending its way north out of the Southwest.

The horse appeared among the Shoshonis about 1670, probably by dint of trade with the Utes, and the effects were galvanic. From the earliest acquisition along the Bear River, the horse spread to the rest of the Shoshonis within a single generation, changing their hunting methods, broadening horizons, and heightening the importance of warfare. Before the advent of the horse, the Shoshonis had hunted buffalo with techniques developed in the Great Basin for killing rabbits. The method involved every member of the tribe in huge drives, stampeding the animals into an increasingly constricted funnel between waving participants and natural bluffs, before trapping them in long nets—a cliff being the accepted substitute for nets when applying the technique to buffalo. With the horse, even a single man could safely pursue and kill the shaggy beast, should the need arise, and the meat and hide of any animal could be carried to camp, rather than constantly moving the camp to keep up with the drift of game. The horse broadened diet along with horizons; now the Shoshonis could amble over to the Snake River country to do a little salmon fishing or harvest the succulent camass bulbs.

Some of the Shoshonis drifted north beyond the Missouri to show off the new "elk dog" that made a man swift as a deer and strong as a grizzly—and used it to settle some old scores among the Blackfeet. Traditionally, combat had been a matter of gathering in two opposing lines, setting up tough, bull-hide shields that were impervious to any available weapons, and hurling insults and a few arrows back and forth until both sides got tired and went home victorious. It was a method suited to the essentially peaceable Shoshonis, but this time they cheated by riding straight into a Piegan camp, whacking a few of the dumbfounded warriors (who had never before seen a horse), and racing back out again.

The furious Piegans responded by recruiting some Assiniboine neighbors who had recently acquired an amazing weapon from a French-Canadian trapper; it made a deafening noise, but left a devastating hole in anything it hit. The allies tracked down a band of Shoshonis who had no horses, issued a challenge, lined up as usual, and then shot holes in the Shoshoni shields and Shoshoni warriors. Following up their advantage, the Piegans fell on another Shoshoni village, but this time found everyone sick or dead, their bodies covered with running sores and scabs. The Piegans took the horses, everything portable, and returned home—only to find themselves ravaged by the fever that consumed their enemies. In one brief exchange the Indians had introduced themselves to the wonders and horrors of a civilization whose outriders still had not reached them. They had ridden the white man's horse, felt the fire and dull pain of his weapons, and watched the insatiable appetite for death of his smallpox.

The horse had changed the role of warfare on the Plains, lifting it beyond the confines of a quasi-ceremonial recreation where few were hurt, to a requisite activity for maintaining the territorial imperative against a world where distances had suddenly shrunk and everyone's horizons were wider. Besides, now when an Indian made war, there was always the chance of stealing the other fellow's horses. The Shoshonis, though well mounted, were without guns, and in short order were pushed back to their mountains and valleys along the Seedskeedee, secured there by the Crows, who held the eastern slopes of the Wind Rivers, and the Blackfeet to the north.

In the course of two centuries, the Shoshonis who made their home in rendezvous country had grown and changed so dramatically that—but for language—they would be unrecognizable to the cousins they left behind in the Great Basin. They were denizens of the buckskin culture, mounted warriors rich beyond belief, who had dramatically changed their styles of eating, dressing, and traveling. But the changes ran even deeper than surface appearances: the Shoshonis had also adopted the social organization and ethics of the Plains. They had, in short, become more like their Crow and Blackfoot enemies, and less like their basin relatives.

The Crows—and now the Shoshonis as well—functioned as warrior societies. It was undeniably a man's world, with women subservient in every aspect of life, and a man measured his worth by accomplishments in essentially violent arts. A man didn't fight simply to protect his family and village; he fought, often with foolish bravado, to acquire prestige by counting coups upon his enemies—that is, striking an armed adversary with a stick or quirt and living to tell the tale, or stealing a horse that was tied to an enemy's tipi. He went on horse-stealing raids in order to garner enough wealth to give it away freely, and thereby be known as a generous man

among his people. And he continued to fight to maintain his status, for to quit before old age withered his limbs was to be a gelding. To enhance his effectiveness as a warrior, he fasted to bring on visions that would offer special insights or amulets to aid in supplications to the proper deities. The entire course of his life, from childhood to senility, focused on proving and improving his effectiveness as a fighter—and it was his skill at the martial arts which rendered him an accomplished hunter, the only other obligation a man had.

While the men fought and hunted in grand style, it was women who did all the work. They prepared the food, raised the children (except for instruction in war, hunting, and religion), made the clothes, and when the men decided it was time, broke camp, loaded the horses, and re-erected the village on a new site selected by the men. In the course of a buffalo hunt, the men rode out in a brief and frenzied flurry of killing, then returned to sit by the tipi reminiscing over what a fine job they had done. Meanwhile the women dressed out the bison, skinned the carcasses, and hauled everything usable back to camp. There a woman roasted ribs and hump for her family, cut the remainder of the meat into strips, and hung it on a willow framework over an open fire to dry. While the meat dried, she scraped the hides down, treated them with a mixture of brain and bone marrow for tanning, pegged them down to dry, and later smoked them over a slow fire. As the meat dried, she pounded much of it to powder, mixing it with serviceberries and chokecherries she had gathered; then she packed this winter's supply of pemmican away in leather bags sealed with tallow. Returning to the hides, she soaked and stretched them to suppleness before stitching them together with sinew and tendon she had stripped from the carcass. Punching holes with a crude awl, and softening the sinew in her mouth as she worked, she fashioned leggings, hunting jerkins, winter robes, dresses, and moccasins. In addition, the women were charged with gathering the prairie flax, mint, and sage that seasoned meals and made teas, and with digging up the balsam and thistle roots, yams, and cow parsnips that added variety to the fare of buffalo, antelope, deer, mountain sheep, and rodent meat that the men provided.

However drudgerous or indolent the life of Indians in rendezvous country, it was an existence expressed and affirmed by the natural world. They were late arrivals on the land, surviving and prospering by Nature's beneficence, and they acknowledged this indebtedness by taking only what they perceived as their share. Nature's supremacy and ultimate wisdom was reflected in an essentially animistic religion; the deities that affected every phase of their lives appeared in the form—and often with the characteristics—of animals that shared their world. It was Coyote, the trickster, who created them, the Geese who brought on the great flood, and Cottontail who restored the sun to its rightful place and created the moon. The world was a balanced and ordered place, with a spot in it reserved for man. What they saw in the world was what they needed—what they received was what they deserved.

A man who walks in moccasins develops an awareness, an appreciation, a sensitivity for the shape and texture of his world. He constantly feels, as well as sees, the land that spawned and succors him, and he seldom forgets that sensation. The prints of the moccasin were shallow, marks that mingled comfortably with the tracks of the other live things in rendezvous country, leaving no permanent scars.

The Mountain Man

In the first blush of the exuberant years that became the white man's nineteenth century, the land that was the center of the world to the Crows and Shoshonis remained a nebulous region of *terra incognita* to peoples who liked to call themselves civilized. To cartographers creating imaginary geography in lofty sanctuaries on the sunrise side of the Mississippi, it was little more than an errant and hopeful twitch of the pen; to the Hudson's Bay Company, with over a century of wilderness experience in North America, it lay beyond the fragile fringe of a growing presence in the Northwest; and to the rough-hewn St. Louis entrepreneurs who looked to the west for their fortunes, it was just another unknown quantity far to the south of the accessible lands that flanked the Missouri and Yellowstone.

For nearly two decades after Lewis and Clark returned to tell America what they had seen in the Stony Mountains, the situation remained largely unchanged. But, within two years after the fur trade began to revitalize in 1822, Ameri-cans were coursing the rivers and streams of this once-remote region, learning the shape of the land, and sharing intimately in its every mood. Out of this encounter between determined men and a unique land would emerge an entirely new approach to the fur trade, a system of logistics and commerce whose trademark became the rendezvous. And out of this system and this land would emerge an American heroic arche-type of almost mythical proportions—the moun-tain man.

On the surface of it, the mountain man ap-peared to be only the functionary-in-the-field of a growing and profitable fur trade. But because of the system that developed, he came to be a permanent resident in the wilderness, and sur-vival supplanted profit as his first consideration. He became a complex of the skills, reactions, and judgments that the land required of him— and he emerged as the penultimate frontiers-man, the yardstick by which all who followed would be measured.

For the mountain man the fur trade became

less a business than a way of life. He could never completely escape the economics of the trade (he was often a victim more of the marketplace than of the elements), but he tuned the whole rhythm of his life to the land, mapping its surface in his mind, measuring its demands in his reflexes, and tempering its malevolence with his adaptability. His ways, like the Indians', became a part of the land—for in the final analysis he was answerable only to his own skills and susceptible only to the world he chose to walk.

The era of the rendezvous and a trade centered in the land of the Seedskeedee did not materialize for nearly twenty years after white men first set out to harvest the rich fur crop of the Rockies. In 1806, even as Lewis and Clark drifted down the Missouri en route home from their transcontinental trek, individual trappers were making their way to the mountains. Two such men, Joe Dickson and Forest Hancock, encountered the explorers and induced a restless hunter from the government party, John Colter, to return upriver with them. Colter led his partners back toward the mountains, paddling up the Yellowstone, which he and Clark had so recently descended, to the streams that rise in the Absaroka mountains. The partnership soon dissolved, probably under the pressure of that winter malady known as cabin fever, but summer found each of the three headed separately downriver toward St. Louis with the season's catch. Dickson and Hancock made it, but once again Colter was intercepted and turned back—this time by a St. Louis merchant named Manuel Lisa, who meant to enter the lucrative fur business in a big way.

Lisa's Missouri Fur Company was organized to tap the fur resources of the Rockies in the traditional manner. Forts would be erected at strategic locations along the major rivers, to which the Indians would bring their furs to trade for the goods of an industrial society. This was the traditional approach to fur gathering, officially recognized by the government. Most of those engaged in the business were traders, not trappers—which was convenient since whites were forbidden by federal law from trapping in the Indian country. Colter and mountain men like him simply ignored a law that originated too far away to be enforced. Long conditioned to think of the West in terms of river travel, Lisa and his contemporaries naturally stuck to the upper Missouri and its principal tributaries. As a consequence, whites came into contact with the Seedskeedee only briefly and peripherally.

In November of 1807, Lisa established his first post where the Bighorn joins the Yellowstone and immediately dispatched Colter to drum up business among any Indians he could find. Colter set off on a thousand-mile hike that took him south to the wintering grounds of the Crows in the upper Wind River Valley. The details of his journey cannot be known for certain, but it is apparent that he crossed the Wind River Range via Union Pass, which led him into the headwater country of the Seedskeedee—the first white man to set foot in the land that would make fur trade history.

The next men to see this land weren't looking for it—they were on the run. A new partner of Lisa's, Andrew Henry, had established a trading post near the Three Forks in the heart of Blackfoot country, hoping to split his time between trapping and trading. But the Blackfeet quickly killed three of his men, establishing a pattern of relations that would persist to the end of the mountain fur business. The pressure continued until his employees began to desert and Henry was forced to decamp, running south to a fork of the Snake that has since borne his name. In the spring of 1811, with his band fragmented and worn, Henry made his way east, apparently crossing the upper reaches of the Seedskeedee, but concerned more with survival than the potential of the countryside.

Three of this ill-fated group, Edward Robinson, John Hoback, and Jacob Rezner, were bound for St. Louis when they met Wilson Price Hunt, who was headed for John Jacob Astor's grand enterprise at the mouth of the Columbia. The trio offered to guide Hunt's band of sixty-five along a route that would avoid the Blackfeet and provide a navigable link to the lower Columbia as well. Hunt agreed and they set out across the plains, finally reaching Union Pass and the Seedskeedee. He was on the lookout for potential fur country, so the possibilities of the region could not have escaped him, but circumstances were to distract his memory.

After Henrys Fork met the Snake, the river turned mean, with formidable canyons and rapids that completely demolished Hunt's plans. The party staggered overland instead, and though they reached Astoria safely, it was obvious that the route was not feasible. Considering the experience of the latter portion of the journey, Hunt may not have harbored particularly rosy memories of his brief passage in the Seedskeedee. Another band of Astorians, this time under Robert Stuart, also passed through the valley and was similarly unimpressed.

The determined warfare of Indians, coupled with a redirection of national attention caused by the War of 1812, forced the traders to withdraw from the upper Missouri. Thus began a ten-year hiatus in the mountain fur trade, but the early years which so tentatively introduced the white man to the future center of the trade had laid a foundation of habit on which it would rise again, although dramatically changed.

It was an advertisement placed in the St. Louis *Enquirer* during March of 1822 by one William Ashley that revived the mountain fur trade after a decade-long quiescence. Ashley stated his proposition in simple terms:

TO

Enterprising Young Men

The subscriber wishes to engage ONE HUNDRED MEN to ascend the river Missouri to its source, there to be employed for one, two, or three years. For particulars enquire of Major Andrew Henry, near the Lead Mines, in the County of Washington, (who will ascend with, and command the party) or to the subscriber at St. Louis.

/s/ Wm. H. Ashley

Out of this venture would grow the fur trade as Americans like to remember it: an innovative system of rendezvous, supply caravans, and mountain men—independent and irascible free trappers living in the wild in a triumphant state of nature.

It is convenient to credit Ashley as being a man of tremendous insight and vision, who recognized the unique demands of the land and the trade, and crafted a system to fit them. In reality the metamorphosis was a gradual one, brought on by circumstance; Ashley was simply a man sufficiently adaptable to find a way around obstacles that stood between him and financial success.

Initially, Ashley's enterprises relied on the traditional elements of river transport and forts. His only departure was the organization of brigades of white men to do the trapping—why waste time cultivating trade relations with often fickle Indians? During his first year Ashley lost a boatload of supplies to the river and fifty horses to raiding Assiniboines, but he did get Henry established on the upper river—where he was promptly attacked by Blackfeet. The following year the Aricaras attacked his spring supply boat, killed fifteen of his men, and turned the party back. Changes were in order.

Ashley dispatched Henry overland to the Yellowstone country during the late summer of 1823 in a last-ditch effort to gain a hold in the traditional fur grounds. Hedging his bets, he sent another party under young Jedediah Smith and Tom Fitzpatrick westward towards the headwaters of the Bighorn, there to make the most of what they might find.

The crossing was a difficult one, traversing the Dakota badlands and the tangled canyons of the Black Hills. Smith was badly mangled by a grizzly, and at one point the entire party very nearly perished from thirst. Shortly after passing the headwaters of Powder River, Edward Rose renewed acquaintance with a band of Crows, who offered to the tattered crew the hospitality of their winter quarters near the source of Wind River. Smith and company had reached the edge of rendezvous country.

It would become axiomatic among the mountain men that Crow women made the best wives. In addition to exceptional beauty, they were happy, chatty, kept a tidy home, fashioned some of the finest buckskins and moccasins extant, and labored long and hard to satisfy the foibles of their men. All of these qualities the Crow women extended to their guests, making the time of winter lodge a pleasurable respite for the Americans.

But the impatient fur seekers needled their hosts relentlessly about what lay where, how to get there, and what they might find. The Crows obliged, regaling the Americans with tales of the Seedskeedee, where a man could leave his traps in the panniers and harvest beaver with a club. They also told of a pass to the south that led through the mountains west of where the Sweetwater rose. Fired more by enthusiasm than by good sense, Smith and his band set off down the Wind River in February, long before any hint of spring. It was a discomforting mistake, as the pumice-dry snows blown at abrasive velocities on the open plains east of the divide quickly wore into their resolve. After William Sublette and James Clyman were nearly lost for good while hunting camp meat, the entire party forted up in a protected canyon near the Sweetwater and fed on the mountain sheep that ranged the cliffs above their camp.

In mid-March Smith and his companions began to suffer from itchy instep—they were vital young men who hadn't yet seen the other side of the mountain. So they cached their excess supplies and moved west toward the pass the Crows had described. Once again the inexperienced party misjudged the rigors of mountain weather. They struggled through six days of frigid winds and bewildering ground blizzards before reaching the mountain gateway. In all likelihood Smith and his men never knew exactly when they crossed the divide, for the wide, gently rolling land of South Pass is almost insignificant in its geography. They had succeeded in crossing the spine of the continent and discovering a pass whose gentle gradient would shape the future history of America; yet to them, the most memorable event of that day came when Clyman managed to kill a buffalo to fill their pinched bellies. Such were the realities of mountain life.

Trailblazing is more than just finding a route; it is also a matter of learning when to use that route. Smith's band had suffered what seemed to be unnecessary hardship, but they were probing into unknown territory. They were doing what every man who trailed the beaver would do later on, and the persistence that led them to dead ends, and into sometimes fatal encounters with the elements would nevertheless open the continent for generations to follow.

Despite difficulties, Smith reached the Green River near Big Sandy River in late March and divided his party for the spring hunt. Jedediah took six men and moved downriver, probably spending most of his time in a rich harvest of Blacks Fork. Fitzpatrick and Clyman, with two others, trapped toward the headwaters in the wake of the spring melt. What each party found was the richest beaver country that trappers would ever encounter in the Rockies—a pelt-

Cathedral Peak in the Wind River Mountains, high along the continental divide, where wind and winter sculpt the face of the land.

hunter's paradise. But while the hunting was good and the weather pleasant, class was always in session in the Rockies; Fitz was about to learn a lesson in mountain morality.

His tiny group was trapping tributary streams when they met a family band of gregarious Shoshonis. Fitz greeted them warmly, fed them sumptuously on beaver, shared camp and companionship, and, naturally but unfortunately, relaxed his vigilance. In the morning the Shoshonis were gone, along with all the horses. Pursuit was impossible, so Fitz continued his trapping on foot, uncomfortable, humiliated, but enlightened by a lesson he was not likely to forget. Returning to meet Smith in June, he unexpectedly encountered his erstwhile guests and seized the opportunity to extemporize some mountain diplomacy. With primed rifles, grim threats, and a dash of bluster, Fitz bartered in the currency that warrior societies understand— and a contrite band of Shoshonis responded by returning his mounts.

When Smith and Fitzpatrick met again on the Sweetwater, Fitz was delegated the task of transporting the season's catch back to civilization in bullboats, the improvised willow-framed and buffalo-skin-covered skiffs of the mountains that looked—and sailed—like washtubs. He was to follow the Sweetwater and North Platte, but the river swamped him near Independence Rock, so he and two others cached the furs there and stumbled the rest of the way on foot, returning with horses early in winter to retrieve the pelts. Jedediah, on the other hand, elected to stay in the mountains, not to build a fort or maintain relations with the Indians, but simply to look at the country and perhaps assay its potential.

Smith and his men were to spend most of the fall and winter in the Snake River country, stirring the ferment of Anglo-American relations merely by their presence—an implied challenge to Hudson's Bay Company suzerainty in the Rocky Mountain reaches of the contested Oregon Country. In the meantime, Ashley was set-

ting out on the expedition that in the end would reshape the form and substance of the American fur trade.

In November of 1824, Ashley left the Missouri settlements with goods to resupply Smith's men, hoping to arrive in the new territory in time for his own band to participate in the spring and summer hunt. But he left with a new plan: finally abandoning river transport, he would rely completely on horses and overland travel. By mid-April he had made his way into the Green River country south of the Sweetwater and South Pass, after a slow and often grueling winter passage across the plains and mountains. It was a learning experience he would not forget.

Ashley split his party for the spring hunt, sending Clyman north toward the familiar headwaters, Zacharias Ham west to unfamiliar country, and Fitzpatrick south to the Uintas (to reach Henrys Fork along the base of the mountains). He took himself down the Green— mainly to find out if it was the famed Buenaventura, the Great River of the West. What Ashley found was Flaming Gorge, for where the river entered the mountains it took on an entirely different aspect as it plunged and twisted through rugged and constricting canyons. He soon convinced himself that little was to be gained either politically or financially by dying on an unnamed western river; he quit his boats in the Uinta basin, acquired horses from the Utes, and made his way in a looping west-by-north arc back toward the appointed meeting place on Henrys Fork.

By now Ashley's men had begun to get the measure of the land, having ranged throughout the upper drainage of the Green as far south as the Uintas. Smith had further expanded their horizons during the winter, ranging across the Bear River region to the west and the beaver-rich waters of the Snake River country, wintering far to the north on the Columbia. In addition to a wealth of furs, the Indians were not uncompromisingly hostile—a factor which had earlier closed the upper Missouri and Three Forks country to Ashley's aspirations. The future was beginning to look brighter.

The scattered bands of Ashley's trappers assembled on Henrys Fork of the Green early in July 1825 to turn over their catch and replenish their outfits from the goods Ashley had caravaned out the previous winter. It was a subdued gathering, as the trappers shared the experiences and information of the last year, enjoyed the luxury of sugared coffee and unrationed tobacco, and stocked up on powder, lead, and traps. Already most of them had decided to stay in the mountains for the fall hunt, counting on Ashley to send another supply train and thereby spare them the long walk to the markets of St. Louis.

Ashley rapidly began to see the logic of the arrangement, for he remembered his own difficult winter crossing of the Plains. Up to now, if a trapping brigade carrying its own supplies hoped to reach the beaver country for the spring and summer hunt, a winter caravan was required. They had already begun to recognize the inferior quality of summer pelts, which meant that any trapping after spring was largely a waste of time and beaver stock. If these men really preferred to stay in the mountains, why not have them rendezvous with a supply train in midsummer, when travel on the Plains was easiest and trapping was at its lowest ebb? That way the trappers could work the streams during the fall as the fur improved, fort up wherever they chose for the winter, and be on hand for the spring thaw. It was a remarkably simple and advantageous system, which made the most of the circumstances and the country. Ashley and his mountain men had learned how to do more than survive; they had adapted themselves and their business to the imperatives of the land, creating a workable symbiosis between man and the mountains.

The system that Ashley first perceived at the gathering on the banks of Henrys Fork in 1825 was refined during the following years into that uniquely American institution, the rendezvous.

Despite its utility, rendezvous became more than a convenient means for trade and resupply; it grew, in time, into a Rocky Mountain fair, a frontier pageant that strutted its way into the national heritage, a brief, bold fiber in the cultural tapestry of the American experience. Rendezvous was celebration in the superlative—bizarre, robust, and profane enough to be a grand piece of mythic folklore, if it hadn't really happened.

The event usually began mundanely enough as trappers straggled along singly and in groups to the site agreed upon the previous year, locations that ranged from Pierre's Hole on the western slope of the Tetons, to Cache Valley and Bear Lake northeast of the Great Salt Lake, to the Popo Agie near the confluence of the Wind and Bighorn rivers, or Hams Fork near its junction with Blacks Fork, and along the wide banks of the Green itself, a few miles above Horse Creek. Whatever the locations, they offered in common an abundance of water, game, and firewood for the trappers and traders, and lush grasslands for their animals.

Ashley's original intention was merely to supply his own brigades of trappers, but even as early as 1826, when his first summer caravan pulled into Cache Valley, the word had spread. Over sixty additional trappers were there waiting to do business, including a batch of deserters from Hudson's Bay Company brigades hoping for a better deal. In the years that followed, rendezvous would come to count its population in the many hundreds, as additional trading companies turned up to compete for the pelts.

The citizens of these instant and ephemeral mountain trading centers represented every element of the fur hunting fraternity: American brigade trappers working under the command of specific companies; Mexicans up from the southern reaches of the Rockies; entire villages of Indians, usually Shoshonis, intent on joining the revelry and trading furs, horses, and women for the miracles of iron and gunpowder; French-Canadians and half-breeds, some refugees from the poor wages of the HBC, others proud inheritors of a century-old tradition of backwoods service as *coureurs de bois* in Canada and the Northwest. But standing tallest of all, bold and independent, was the free trapper—hunting when and where he pleased, selling his furs to the highest bidder, and finding fulfillment in a land where the only law was Nature's. Despite their differences, all the members of this mountain menagerie shared the wilderness life, and through this mutual experience enjoyed an easy rapport. They regaled each other with tales of the past year's exploits and adventures, describing the new country they had seen and speculating over what they hadn't. They compared notes on the ever-fickle mood of Indians they had encountered, and acknowledged with a noncommittal grunt the untimely demise of old acquaintances who had pushed their luck one season too long.

With the arrival of the trade caravans, usually in early July, the trappers began the almost instantaneous disposal of furs that represented a year of arduous and often dangerous labor. Considering the rate of exchange, this wasn't too difficult. Prime beaver was worth about four dollars a pound in the mountains; with an adult pelt weighing in at roughly a pound and a half, the trapper was tossing six-dollar banknotes on the trading blanket—which wasn't a bad price for fur. But the dollar value of pelts was largely academic, in light of the fact that he was paying outrageously inflated prices for supply goods.

As a general rule, what cost the trader one dollar in St. Louis, cost the trapper at least ten in the mountains. At that rate the necessities of life came high: blankets at $20 apiece, lead at $1 per pound, powder at $4 per pound, knives and hatchets between $3 and $6 each, traps at over $20 apiece, and good Hawken rifles at prices approaching three figures. Even simple luxuries like coffee, sugar, and flour retailed at $2 per pint, with tobacco reaching $5 per pound. While the trader may have paid a good price for fur, he was certain never to walk away from a transaction anything less than a big winner. But for the most part mountain men were the sort who placed more value on enjoying life than acquiring a bankroll, and they spent without quibbling. After all, winter might find their scalp adorning a Blackfoot lance; what good was money then?

Even at these inflated rates, acquiring what a mountain man considered necessary seldom consumed even half his pelt pack, and it was then that the trader played his trump card—booze. Alcohol was the fuel that ignited rendezvous, generating the brawling, swaggering, uninhibited behavior that made the event unforgettable. Ashley had come to the mountains dry in 1825, but he and others rectified that oversight in subsequent years, despite a government ban on alcohol in Indian territory. The law had a fatal loophole—it permitted a daily ration of spirits for the keelboatmen who once propelled the supply boats up the Missouri—and the traders simply retained that quaint custom. It got to be downright amazing how many boatmen were needed to shepherd a caravan of pack animals up the Platte River.

What passed for an alcoholic beverage in the mountains was nothing more than pure grain alcohol purchased in St. Louis, cut four or five times with branch water at the rendezvous site, with a little tobacco thrown in for color and flavor. It did, however, have two redeeming qualities: it made a great deal of money for the traders at very slight expense; and it got the mountain men incredibly drunk in very short order, which was what they wanted. The debauch that followed could last a week or more, depending upon how long the pelts lasted.

The trappers fought, caroused, and squandered money, draping their squaw of the year, week, or hour in geegaws and bright cloth. They gambled at "hand," the Indian game of chance that knew a variety of refinements but usually boiled down to nothing more than a drunken version of "Button, Button, Who's Got the Button?" Rough-hewn practical jokes were devised, as when revelers doused a stu-pored comrade with alcohol, touched a match to him, and then howled with delight as he whirled like a flaming dervish through the camp. Shootings erupted, bones were broken, and the year's wages were gambled or frittered away in a few days, but remorse over indiscretion was an emotion seldom seen. The excesses of rendezvous were part of the life, a life the mountain men had created themselves.

The bacchanalian abandon that characterized rendezvous was an almost predictable outgrowth of the business. These were men who chose to live close to the primal side of life, where success was survival, measured in its most elemental terms. Ragged emotion, discomfort, and pain were not relative or ethereal concepts in their world, but real and recognizable absolutes that a man had to cope with every day. They lived under extreme pressure all year, maintaining constant vigilance and almost daily making decisions that determined whether they lived or died. Rendezvous was the one opportunity during the year to let down their defenses and relax, an activity they undertook with the same elemental vigor that typified the rest of their lives.

When the pelts were all traded and the liquor swilled to the last drop, a mountain man, nursing an aching head and an unsteady stomach, often found that in drunken enthusiasm he had gambled away horse, rifle, traps, and supplies for the coming year. It was an odious circumstance, particularly for the free trapper, but one which the traders packing up for the return trip to St. Louis were willing to cure. A quick conference, a pledge of the next year's catch, and the trapper was outfitted and on his way, pointing his moccasins back toward the lonely streams and mountains that were his livelihood and life. He was a mountain man, and there was nowhere else for him to go.

Alfred Jacob Miller:
Impressions of the Wilderness

Alfred Jacob Miller died in 1874, largely unrecognized in his own time for his efforts as an artist. But it is through his perceptive vision and skilled brush that the finest firsthand representations of Rocky Mountain fur trade life have come down to us. Miller was a professional, trained by Thomas Sully and supplementing that solid foundation with a lengthy sabbatical at the *École des Beaux Arts* in Paris.

But the artist's Rocky Mountain renderings are especially striking and incisive because he witnessed the scenes he painted. Unlike many of his contemporaries, whose paintings of the West were products of a facile talent fertilized with romantic secondhand information, Miller took his canvas to the scene and rendered what he saw and felt.

He went west as a member of Captain William Drummond Stewart's hunting, sight-seeing, and adventure-seeking excursion during the halcyon years of the fur trade. He spent 1837 afield, seeing the mountain men and Indians at rendezvous and watching their pursuit of livelihood and survival. The result is a unique collection of drawings, oil paintings, and watercolors that capture not only the substance of life but the mood as well.

Miller worked with a pale palette, and his watercolors exhibit a becoming delicacy that in a lesser painter might have eroded the strength and visceral earthiness of the life he portrayed. In Miller's work, however, the result is a poignant sensitivity and ethereal innocence, which underscore the delicate symbiosis that mountain men and Indians maintained with the land. He was, to give him the highest accolade possible, an artist who knew his subject.

THE BEAVER MEN

"The Lost Trapper." *In the wilderness, man is never more vulnerable than when he doesn't know which way to run.*

"Trappers." The self-reliant Men-in-Nature take their ease.

"Antoine Clement." *Clear-eyed and strong-boned,
one of the hundreds who opened the West.*

"Pierre" (left), *an otherwise anonymous trapper, was rendered in a seemingly uncharacteristic reflective pause, perhaps opening a new door on the image of the perpetual man-of-action, while* "Louis—Mountain Trapper" *strikes a more traditional, heroic pose.*

TRAILING
THE
BEAVER

"In the Rocky Mountains." *The essential quality of an overnight camp survives the misty intrusion of a Hudson River School haze on the high mountain air.*

87

"Trappers Starting for Beaver Hunt." *The mechanics of trapping dictated small groups, a circumstance which sat well with most mountain men.*

"The Lost 'Green-Horn.'" *Abroad and lost in a flat, featureless plain, a tenderfoot was at the mercy of his own initiative. It was the Rocky Mountain College, and a passing grade was getting to see the sun rise again.*

"Setting Traps for Beaver." *Men worked alone
or paired in the half-light of dusk and
dawn to set and retrieve their traps, wading
the chill waters into a lifetime of rheumatism.*
"Trappers Around a Campfire" *(right) savored
the relief from a day's work and tensions.*

"Bull Boating on the Platte River." *Buffalo hides*
stretched over a willow-branch frame provided
an ungainly craft that was vulnerable to upset,
but it was usually the driest option available.

Bull — Boating
the Platte River

"Captain Joseph Reddeford Walker—A Bourgeois and His Squaw."
A near-legendary figure in the trade, Walker—like many of his colleagues
—took a woman to wife who was suited to his life-style.

"Hunting the Bear" (*above*) *and* "Breaking Trail to Escape from Indians" (*right*)
illustrated a life fraught with peril, but one that men chose with both eyes open.

GOOD NEIGHBORS,
BAD NEIGHBORS

"Escape from the Blackfeet." Unless the odds were undeniably in his favor, the mountain man would adopt the Indian tactic of running away to fight another day, particularly if the opposition were the implacable Blackfeet.

"Indian Hospitality." *A man took his friends where he found them, understood their values, and respected their rites and rituals if he was to walk their land.*

"Encampment of Snake Indians—Wind River Mountains." *Probably depicting Shoshonis on the western slope of the range, Miller's painting captures the idyllic aura of a life that also featured a generous measure of dreary realism.*

"Indian Encampment."

"Snake Indians Migrating."

"Shoshone Camp Fording River."

"Snake Indian Council." *These mountain conventions fulfilled the desire for meeting old friends and recounting past coups, while sustaining the loose-knit confederation between family bands.*

"Indians Testing Their Bows." *The high-plains and mountain Indians lived within a warrior society, testing themselves and measuring their success in essentially violent arts.*

Indians testing their Bows

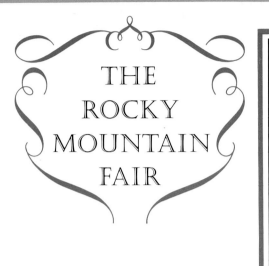

THE
ROCKY
MOUNTAIN
FAIR

"The Greeting." *Companions became friends, and friends became brothers in the sharing of hardship in a lonely land.*

"Indian Procession in Honor of Captain William Stewart."
Full regalia and mock warfare—any occasion became an event.

"Making Presents to Snake Indians." *In the time-
honored tradition of Indian relations, a man demonstrated
his good heart and honest intentions with the produce of an
industrial society.*

"Trapper's Bride." *The bond might be for convenience, self-protection,
or companionship—and occasionally even for love.*

"Moonlight—Camp Scene." *A gathering of the brigade might find a sharing of wisdom, experience, geography, or even a fanciful yarn.*

The Skin Stretched Tight

Rendezvous was the distinguishing characteristic of the American fur trade that evolved on the western slope of the continental divide. It was a necessary adaptation that the land demanded, and in the course of making business possible, rendezvous also made it memorable. But to the mountain man who trailed the beaver, the fur business was one part rendezvous to eleven parts hard work and survival. The festive surrealism of the July debauchery stood in stark contrast to the compelling reality of living from August through June in a wilderness that sometimes seemed deliberately malevolent. It was during those eleven months that the essence of the fur trade was to be found, the time when a mountain man earned his title.

A great many of the trappers who fanned out through rendezvous country—and beyond to the Colorado mountains, the Snake River country to the west, and up north along the Bighorn, Yellowstone, and Three Forks waters—did their hunting in company brigades, working under the direction of master mountain men like Jim Bridger, David Jackson, Tom Fitzpatrick, and William Sublette. The brigades were large, occasionally numbering as many as sixty trappers, and were therefore somewhat unwieldy. But they offered the distinct advantage of being less susceptible to Indian attack—even Blackfeet hesitated to take on a score or more of well-armed mountain men. For actual trapping the brigade was split into smaller groups of three or four men, each group trapping out a small stream for several days before rejoining the main body. The small bands were vulnerable but necessary, for the nature of the business required that men work quietly and unobtrusively.

In contrast to the company brigades, most of the free trappers traveled and hunted in pairs or groups of three and four, counting on stealth and increased mobility to avoid undesirable encounters with the Indians. A few genuine misanthropes like Bill Williams eschewed companionship entirely, rambling the mountains in solitude, responsible only for themselves, not risking the chance that a companion's error would put them in danger. Others, like Edward Rose and Jim Beckwourth, went completely native and spent much of their time living and hunting with their adopted bands of Crows. By disposition and conditioning most mountain men lived, looked, and thought so much like Indians that the transition was hardly noticed. But no matter how he traveled to the trapping grounds, every mountain man evolved as a self-contained, self-sustaining complex of equipment, skills, and sensitivities necessary to survival and hunting success.

The familiar figure of the buckskin-clad trapper was an image born in necessity and not universally true. When they were available, woolen pants and shirt were preferred—wool was warmer and stayed fairly warm even when wet—but a few months' hard use usually shredded the fabric. Buckskin was more durable and turned a thorn better, but it wasn't very warm, stretched into sagging folds when wet, shrunk too tight when drying, and hardened into a stiff, abrasive annoyance that chafed every joint. But it was available, and often a trapper could purchase his hunting-shirt, leggings, and moccasins from Indian women, thereby avoiding the bother of making them himself. A heavy blanket capote usually completed his wardrobe, serving double duty as overcoat and bedroll.

While his garb often reflected what was available, his other equipment was selected to make him self-sufficient; little was carried that was not absolutely essential for survival. In his belt he carried a small hatchet and a heavy skinning knife, both of which could function either as tool or weapon. A favored knife of the later years was manufactured on the banks of the Green River in Massachusetts and stamped "GR" on the blade just below the handle. From it derived the trapper's expression "up to Green River," meaning to sink a blade clear to the

manufacturer's stamp on the hilt, or more broadly, to go all the way in any endeavor. Also dangling from his belt was an awl for making repairs to his clothes, a mold for running rifle balls, and a wire worm for cleaning heavily leaded and powder-caked barrels.

Around his neck hung his "possibles sack," containing pipe and tobacco, "medicine" for baiting traps, a few spare parts for the lockwork of his rifle, and maybe even a Jew's harp. Another pouch for lead balls and flints hung at his side, along with a powder horn. When he could afford and obtain one, the preferred weapon was a heavy, half-stocked rifle made by the Hawken brothers of St. Louis, normally firing a half-ounce ball of about .54 caliber, fast enough to be reliably lethal within a range of about two hundred yards. While Hawken rifles were generally accounted the best, a trapper a thousand miles from St. Louis often had to get by with something less—even settling for the smaller caliber smooth-bore fusees made by the British for the Indian trade.

The mountain man's pack animal carried a sack of traps, a quantity of flour and salt, perhaps a kettle, and usually some tobacco and trade goods for that chance meeting with a band of Indians who hadn't quite decided whether they were hostile or not. Some trappers favored mules as draft animals, mainly because they were harder for Indians to run off in a raid, and a lot of Indians wouldn't go out of their way to steal one. Horses were reassuring—they were fast if you had to make a lightning getaway—but as often as not they were the very magnets that drew the hostiles in the first place.

But the mountain man was more than his animals and gear: he was a creature in tune with the world he inhabited, knowing what to do and when to do it, and equipped with the skills to carry it out. Alone in the wilderness, he was his own cook, surgeon, soldier, wrangler, guide, seamstress, veterinarian, and gunsmith, and he had to be competent in each role. When trapping, he either did it right or caught no beaver and lost his traps in the bargain; either he knew how to care for his stock, or he found himself afoot; and if he failed to protect camp-goods and cache properly, the wolverines and grizzlies spread his pelts and food from horizon to horizon. He had to be able to read a track and from it divine direction, speed, number, and the relative worth or danger of its maker to him. A twig bent out of place, a hawk startled from its roost, a scent on the wind, or the gathering of clouds at sunset might all hold meaning for him—he had to decide which to heed or ignore. When he found himself in the middle of nowhere without gun, knife, flint, or horse, and usually with Indians howling down his neck—as John Colter, Hugh Glass, William Sublette, or Osborne Russell did on various occasions—he had to be able to feed, warm, and defend himself with nothing more than bare hands and his wits.

A man who chose the mountain life had to be judicious, for if he tried to substitute muscle for thought once too often—if he went "up to Green River" when the knife should have been in the sheath—he would be nothing more than a memory come next rendezvous. He had to be able to judge when not to push his luck with the weather, or how badly he really wanted grizzly meat. Where Indians were concerned, he had to decide whether to run, bluster, or attack; to most mountain men a fight avoided was a victory won. Because Indians would seldom fight unless the odds were decidedly in their favor, trappers usually found it wise to avoid a band on the prod. Occasionally mountain men would pick a fight with Indians—out of vengeance, a need to "teach the pesky varmints a lesson," or just for the hell of it (as at the Pierre's Hole rendezvous in 1832, when the revelers raced out to scrap with a migrating band of Gros Ventres who were minding their own business)—but they were always careful to employ the Indians' tactic. A man learned from whomever he could in the mountains.

There were some men who managed to last in the trade with less than superlative abilities, working in the brigades and letting men like Sublette, Smith, and Bridger do most of the thinking. But even these had a mastery of the basic skills and either a need that was fulfilled by the mountain life or a personality that could not be reconciled to civilization. The money to be made in the business did not justify any other kind of man. To survive required a talent for learning quickly and the senses, strength, and disposition for the task—otherwise a man died or ran for home. While a man might pick the mountain life, the mountains also picked the man, inexorably eliminating those who could not measure up.

As with every other creature of this wilderness, the cycle of the mountain man's life was governed by the seasons. He may have been the most efficient and adaptable predator at large, but like the grizzly, the wolf, the hawk, or the weasel, his existence was timed to the rhythm of the elements. The weather controlled both him and his prey, dictating when to hunt and when to hole up, offering comfort and abundance at times, and at others testing his mettle as it withered or froze. In rendezvous country the land and its weather were the forces to be reckoned with, and man had to accommodate himself to them.

When rendezvous began to break up, usually by mid-July, the warmth of summer still lay heavy on the land. Unless a trapper intended to hunt far to the north above the Missouri, or south toward the Spanish villages of Taos and Santa Fe, or even to seek out the coastal lands near Pacific waters, he did not need to hurry. In summer's heat the beaver had shed the rich coat that made a prime, high-priced pelt. The trapper would have to wait for the returning cold before the animals began to put on the soft underfur that was ideal for felting. In brigades, in pairs, or alone, the mountain men packed their gear and began a leisurely return to favored hunting grounds.

Wherever they went, they headed for the high country. It was there that the cold returned the earliest and the pelts would be the most valuable. The trapper followed rivers, creeks, and tiny streams, seeking out the mountain meadows and gentle gradients rich in aspen and willow where beaver liked to build their dams and lodges or to nest under the banks. A single hunter usually worked a half-dozen traps, so he was looking for concentrations of animals rather than the lone beaver on four miles of creek.

Trapping was a refined art, but one that knew no preordained, inflexible method. The circumstances of stream bed, bank, water force and volume, surrounding foliage, prevalent predators, and local climate combined to create an almost infinite variety of situations—each one taxing the hunter's skill in setting his traps. The mountain man preferred to set his line in the evening, when the gathering darkness offered a measure of safety from Indians. He looked first for runways, where beaver habitually entered and left the water, but most of his sets involved baiting a trap and drawing the beaver to it. Working in the half-gloom of dusk, the trapper forsook the relative comfort of the banks for the chilling cold of the stream, because the water masked the man-scent that would warn off these supremely wary animals. Wading to a suitable site, he set the trap about four inches under the surface, scraping and shaping the bottom for proper depth and freedom of action for the trap jaws. When baiting, a succulent willow wand was stabbed into the bank and arched out over the trap; daubed with castoreum, the extract of beaver sexual glands, it was an enticing attraction. Rising to sniff or taste the twig, a beaver's feet drove down onto the trip-pan, and he was caught.

But snaring a beaver and keeping it could often be two different matters. Despite the fact that traps weighed upwards of five pounds, a healthy adult could drag one onto land, gnaw off the clamped foot, and escape. To prevent this the mountain man ran the trap chain into deep water, driving in a dry stake to secure it. A beaver thus prevented from taking the trap to dry ground would dive in terror for the remembered security of deep water, where the weight of trap and chain would hold him until he drowned. If his struggles pulled the stake loose, it would float, marking the trap's location.

The trapper returned to his line in the half-light of dawn, retrieved his traps, and quickly skinned the animals before returning to camp. During the daylight hours he faced the task of dressing the pelts. This was a dull chore that nonetheless required care and was sufficiently time-consuming that it effectively limited his traps to six. The skin had to be scraped clean of all tissue and membrane, and then stretched on a willow hoop to dry for several days before being stamped with the trapper's mark, folded, and packed. The furs had to be protected from downpours—a difficult task when living in the open—and periodically aired and shaken. If a hunter worked with a brigade this dressing of his furs was often handled by greenhorns or camp-tenders. If he maintained a squaw, it was her job. Otherwise he did it himself.

The trapper continued his work through the fall, all the while hunting his own meat, cooking, relocating camp constantly (as much to avoid detection by Indians as to find beaver), maintaining his gear, and always on guard against the mistake that would leave him injured, afoot, unarmed, or bald. The streams were worked down from the higher elevations as winter approached, until by November most of the streams were frozen, the beaver had taken to their lodges beneath the ice, and it was time for a mountain man to find his own winter lodge.

Brigades normally hung together for the winter, seeking out the lowlands and protected valleys where the wind's force might be cut, feed would remain for their mounts, and game to fill the winter pot would congregate. A man with an Indian wife would occasionally seek out her people for winter companionship, but just as often they would find him, moving in to share his robes, eat his food, and make an uproar of his hibernation. He could mend clothing and repair traps, or watch his woman do it while she gabbled incessantly in a language he might or might not fully understand. Responsibilities were few, and his only chore, if he had a squaw, was to keep meat in the pot. Sometimes camp would have to be moved to keep his animals in feed, but real dedication was given to resting his body and catching up on his sleep. Winter was a time for lounging by the fire and watching the smoke tan the lodge-skins for next year's leggings and moccasins.

All too soon winter would begin to break; the howling winds would be replaced by chinooks that swept the snow and chill from the valleys. The lower waters would reappear as the ice stretched, popped, and rumbled in the thaw, and it would be time to return to trapping, for now was when the fur lay heaviest on the beaver, cultivated by a winter of chill waters. The hunters followed the thaw during the spring, trapping higher into the mountains until the fur got thin and it was time to find their way to rendezvous.

It was a demanding life they followed, and for many of them a brief one. Much of the time it seemed to be a life of feast or famine, a rule by extremes in every aspect: it was either plenty of fat cow or starvation; incredible cold or stupefying heat; when the hunting was good there were beaver to burn, and then luck would turn and they lost not only the pelts, but traps, horses, and guns as well. It was not a world the meek would inherit, for only the strong, the alert, and the adaptable survived. Those trappers who survived several decades invariably carried the scars of fights and mishaps, the limps and twisted limbs of broken bones not properly set, and the rheumatism and arthritis that were the reward for thousands of hours spent wading in icy streams.

In 1826, when the fur trade in rendezvous country was still a young industry, William Ashley quit the mountains and returned to St. Louis to pursue a checkered political career and to make a fortune buying and selling furs rather than trapping them. He sold out to Jedediah Smith, David Jackson, and William Sublette, whose firm would spend the next four years trying to show a profit. They succeeded finally, in spite of the fact that Sublette spent most of his time traveling between rendezvous and civilization, or securing capital and stalling creditors in St. Louis; and in spite of Smith, who spent two years tramping across the Great Basin, California, and most of the Pacific Northwest in expensive and profitless exploration. The real hero of the company was Jackson, who dutifully went about trapping, unsung by any chronicler, until the business was out of debt. Little is known of the man, his work, or his travels—although his name survives in one of Wyoming's most beautiful holes.

Smith, Jackson, and Sublette survived the growing years of the trade, when trappers began to reach into every corner of the mountain West, and they sold out in 1830 to the Rocky Mountain Fur Company. The RMF was a partnership of Jim Bridger, Tom Fitzpatrick, Milton Sublette (younger brother of William), Henry Fraeb, and John Baptiste Gervais, and if a monopoly on mountain expertise and experience could make money, the RMF would have been an unqualified success. But none of the partners was a businessman, and although they led brigades that trapped phenomenal numbers of beaver, they were repeatedly victimized by suppliers and St. Louis businessmen. In addition, the field was getting crowded with competitors eager to share in what appeared to be a lucrative business. By 1832 the rendezvous at Pierre's Hole was already swollen with trapping and trading concerns: Rocky Mountain Fur, Astor's revived American Fur Company, Gault and Blackwell of St. Louis, Nathaniel Wyeth (a Boston iceman trying his hand with a brigade),

a group out of Taos, and an infantry captain on leave named Benjamin Bonneville who sometimes acted as if he were doing more scouting and plotting for the government than trapping for himself.

The fierce competition among the Americans was extended to the British; the HBC, fearful of losing traditional trapping grounds in a settlement of the Oregon question, was hunting heavily to get what it could before being pushed out. The beaver population, once harvested carefully to insure that some were left for seed stock, began to diminish alarmingly. Compounding the problem was a shift in the world of fashion—silk began to replace beaver felt as the most desirable material for hats. The price of beaver, of course, dropped immediately, and companies in the field had to trap even harder to pay their debts. In only a few years this sickening, self-consuming downward spiral had reduced a beaver population, once thought to be inexhaustible, to near extinction.

By 1840 it was all over. The rendezvous that year, held at the historic site on the Green above Horse Creek, was a dismal affair—a quiet and sullen wake for the passing of an era. Few furs changed hands, and there was nothing extra for drinking or gambling. One mountain man, lamenting the situation, described his lot: "Now the mountains are so poor that one would stand a right good chance of starving if he were obliged to hang up here for seven days. The game is all driven out. No place here for a white man now. Too poor, too poor. What little we get, you see, is bull beef. Formerly, we ate nothing but cows, fat and young. More danger then, to be sure; but more beaver, too; and plenty of grease about the buffalo ribs. Ah! those were good times; but a white man has now no more business here."

What would become of the mountain men, who knew nothing but the life they had led? Now not only was their means of livelihood gone, but the pristine wilderness they had ruled was beginning to get crowded with strangers looking over the country and headed for Oregon. Some of the old trappers gave up and returned to the states, accepting the civilization they had once so haughtily defied. Some, like Joe Meek, had gone on to Oregon to learn how the next stage of civilizing a frontier worked. Others simply moved farther back into the wild, to eke out an existence in solitude. But geography had been the foundation of the trade— no one knew the mountains better than a trapper—and a few put this knowledge to work for the new arrivals. Fitzpatrick guided the first wagon train to California through its Rocky Mountain passage and later became the first Indian agent for the Upper Platte district, probably one of the best men who ever filled the post, and certainly the most qualified. Kit Carson gained fame as the guide for Frémont on his "pathfinding" explorations. Jim Bridger split his time between managing an emigrant re-supply and repair post on the Oregon Trail and guiding for the army, where he gained a reputation as a coward among some young officers because he clung to the mountain man's prudent dictum that you didn't fight Indians until the odds were decidely in your favor.

They were men suited to the mountains, who came to know the country better than any white men before or since. While the fur trade prospered, they lived as a part of the land, contributing to the whole, and were shaped by it themselves. But through their experience they eroded its sanctity and unveiled its mysteries. They made it comprehensible and available to people less interested in learning the lessons a wilderness has to teach. By their knowledge the mountain men had opened their home to new eras and different concepts—eras and concepts incompatible with and destructive to their own.

Strangers on the Slopes

In the years after 1840, when both the beaver population and the commercial value of the fur had declined far enough to put the trappers out of business and end the rendezvous forever, a fur trade of sorts continued to flourish in the West. But the emphasis was on buffalo robes— a bonanza opened up by a new tanning process that rendered the leather ideal for use as drive belts for industrial machinery—and the few buffalo herds west of the divide had disappeared around 1840. The skin game had moved onto the Plains and back to the upper Missouri River country, and the land that once rattled with the energy and activity of trappers and rendezvous seemed destined for a return to the primeval quiet.

For over two decades much of rendezvous country remained the home of the Shoshonis, the mountain Crows, and a few solitary trappers who could not give up the old ways and eked out a living on winter fur. But across the center of the basin, trending southwest from South Pass, an uncharacteristic tumult continued un-

abated. It was a great river of humanity, not flowing to anywhere in rendezvous country, but heading beyond toward California and Oregon, the twin beacons of Manifest Destiny. Some would pause just beyond the Wasatch to carve out an empire with grit and determination at the edge of the Salt Lake wastelands, and some of these same people would try their hand in rendezvous country; but for most of the transients the region was only a barrier land to be endured en route to greener pastures.

The mountain men may have had a premonition of this cavalcade at the 1836 rendezvous near the confluence of Horse Creek and the Green. Arriving in the supply train with the traders was Marcus Whitman, who had carved an arrowhead out of Bridger's back the year before and had generally shown himself to be a man who could pull his own weight and was therefore to be respected, even if he was a little too temperate in his habits to be one of the boys. This time he brought with him Henry Spaulding and, of all things, two white women. Eliza Spaulding was too shriveled and sick from the overland journey to excite much interest, but Narcissa Whitman was bright, energetic, and almost painfully beautiful—especially to men who had been in the wilderness for several years. Narcissa charmed and bedazzled the trappers, but not so much so that they missed the significance of these first women across the divide: women meant families, and families meant permanent settlement, and that meant growing numbers of emigrant wagons across and beyond the beaver country.

During the 1840s and 1850s the tide of emigrants grew to exceed even the howling nightmares of antisocial mountain men, and from the time the grass first greened on the prairie until snow-clogged passes closed down the trail in winter, the swaying procession continued. John Charles Frémont, while ostensibly on an expedition to encourage migration by mapping the Oregon Trail, noted in his journal that a ribbon of white-topped Conestogas stretched in both directions from his vantage point, and the number of emigrants in evidence was already large. The Indians were equally impressed by the numbers, and perhaps even a little frightened, but not to the degree that they waged unrelenting war on every passing wagon train. Conflicts were rare, despite the assumptions of popular fiction, and the Shoshonis recognized that these wagon people were only a temporary nuisance heading west to bully somebody else out of their land. One Shoshoni even saw a blessing in the migration, suggesting that his tribesmen go east and settle in the great empty expanse of land the whites had left.

The migration was possible because South Pass, near the southeastern tip of the Wind River Range, is unlike the steep, narrow defiles that are commonly recognized as mountain passes. It is a broad, open stretch of grass and sagebrush that rises to the continental divide in a gradient gentle enough for horse-drawn wagons to negotiate. The trail led across the almost indistinguishable divide, down Little Sandy Creek to its junction with the Big Sandy, and from there to a crossing of the Green. The route continued southwesterly to Blacks Fork before turning northwest to Bear River, which it followed around the northern end of the Wasatch Range.

Life on the trail was hard. A necessarily bland diet was complicated by water so alkaline that it was often unpalatable and, when it could be drunk, inevitably gave rise to rumbling bowels and uneasy digestion. Grass was scarce for draft animals; the long pull began to break down the horses especially. Dust, wind, and heat were constant companions for the travelers, and iron rims began falling off wheels as spokes shrank and cracked in the dry winds. The journey became an ordeal, with the emigrants alternately cussing the conditions and praying for something better over the next rise.

Jim Bridger, who had been canny enough to lead successful fur brigades for over a decade and come out of it with his hair intact, thought he saw an opportunity in these poor, bedraggled souls. He built a fort on Blacks Fork, where the grasses on the broad river bottom stand knee deep all year round, and hauled a forge, a load of iron, and some supplies out from St. Louis. It was every businessman's dream: the only source of supply in the midst of a crying demand. He spent his summers repairing wagons, refitting wheels, and selling supplies from a price list he had learned at rendezvous. He also traded stock with the emigrants, usually at the rate of one fresh animal for two of their gaunt, spent creatures—which he then fattened up on free grass for the next year's customers.

Other mountain men saw Jim's success in a growing market and built rafts to ferry the emigrant wagons over the Green River crossing. It was a good scheme that earned enough cash money during the brief summer to allow the old

Winter shrouds the desert basin in the land of the Seedskeedee,
a stumbling block in this gateway for a nation moving west.

trappers to remain in their beloved mountains. But their idyll began to crumble after 1851, when most of rendezvous country was included in the newly-created Utah Territory, under the governorship of Brigham Young. It had been only four years since the first Mormons trudged into the Salt Lake valley, but already missionaries and settlers were moving out into the choice river valleys along the Bear and Green rivers—and here was the authority to make that presence supreme.

The new governor naturally assumed that these choice concessions should go to the faithful, and accordingly issued permits for toll bridges. The mountaineers bristled, and the bridge builders scurried back to Salt Lake City. The following year another group of Mormons returned to take over the rafts and managed to ferry a few early wagons before a heavily armed band of trappers making war-talk ran them off again. But Brigham Young was not a man to be trifled with, and he set about ridding himself of the stubborn heathens.

He wanted Bridger's fort on Blacks Fork, but efforts to buy it proved futile, since Jim didn't like these people who insisted on settling on his backyard. Since outlying Mormon settlements were suffering Indian raids, and Bridger sold guns to Indians, Young decided to solve a lot of problems in one swift move. He sent an armed company to run Bridger out and at the same time secure the Green River ferries for the church. They were ultimately successful at both tasks; Brigham wasn't a man to be trifled with.

During the next few years the Mormons held control in rendezvous country, as settlements increased and efforts were made to convert the Lamanites—the Indians, who were, according to Mormon theology, descendants of the lost tribes of Israel. One strategy employed to win the confidence of, and safety from, these Lamanites was to marry Indian girls, a device that quickly evaporated when the Shoshoni chief Washakie agreed, with the proviso that his men could take Mormon brides.

Brigham Young's authority began to crumble in a few years when the national government took umbrage at the shoddy treatment given federal judges and officials in Utah, and the feud boiled over into rebellion. Washington sent a military expedition to reassert federal authority, and while the venture degenerated into a comic opera, the desired result was achieved. But the Mormon presence had been established, especially in small settlements in the western mountain valleys of rendezvous country—a presence that is still strongly felt today.

To one degree or another, the overland migration lasted nearly twenty years, although by the mid-1850s the number making the trek had decreased considerably. But all those years, taken together, could not begin to match the volume of frenzied activity that was about to follow. America had decided to build herself a railroad, and it was going to run right across rendezvous country.

Every westerner smart enough to tie his shoelaces knew that railroads were the engines of Progress, bringing prosperity and civilization to the remotest wilderness the rails blessed; under the benign influence of steel and cross-ties, thriving cities would sprout, industry flourish, the desert bloom, real estate values increase, and everybody would get rich forever and ever. At least that was the prevailing theory. The railroad did cross the Seedskeedee, it did bring a short-lived prosperity, and it did bring civilization of a sort. But its impact on rendezvous country was much less profound than anticipated—largely because the railroad, like the majority of emigrants, was intent on getting through, rather than to, the region.

Under the provisions laid down in the Pacific Railway Act, the Union Pacific received $32,000 in low-interest subsidy loans for each mile of track built through the region, plus title to the odd-numbered sections for twenty miles on either side of the right-of-way—an incentive that worked out to twenty square miles of land for each mile of track. Railroads had traditionally survived the high initial costs of construction only because of the profitable business that naturally accrued from the markets created by the railroad's presence; but with the government subsidies attached to the transcontinental road, very real profits lay in construction as well. Rather than relying on nascent markets, the Union Pacific blazed across the mountain barrier grabbing as much land and subsidy money as possible.

The construction brought a brief boom during 1868, as settlements sprouted along the line to serve the thousands of graders and tracklayers building the railroad. But end of track moved so fast that towns that blossomed overnight often wilted just as fast when the construction gangs moved beyond their reach. A few, like Rock Springs, Green River, and Evanston, put down substantial enough roots to survive, but even they suffered through years of economic doldrums after the flush days of construction had passed.

The throngs of people and instant cities that accompanied the progress of the line barely qualified as civilization. A whole menagerie of gamblers, prostitutes, and portable saloons leapfrogged along the line, feeding on the wages of workmen who had nowhere else to turn for entertainment. This transient den of iniquity, known to the gandy dancers as "Hell on Wheels," carried the kind of wide open atmosphere that fostered lawlessness everywhere it went. Townspeople with a stake in the future usually responded with extralegal measures—a polite euphemism for viligance committees and lynch law.

Bear River City was one of those instant cities that didn't survive, but during the winter of 1868 it was jumping with activity, much of it so violent that vigilantes posted a notice ordering "garroters to vacate this city or hang within

sixty hours from this noon." Seven days later they dragged three men from jail and lynched them; unfortunately one of the trio was a railroad worker, and his compatriots raided the town in retaliation, burning the jail and looting stores. The local law fought back, and in the ensuing gun battle perhaps a dozen people died. The rioters were finally driven from town, but they left with threats to return and burn every building to the ground. Federal troops from Fort Bridger finally restored order by imposing martial law for two weeks.

The building of the Union Pacific also stimulated the beginnings of the logging industry in the region. As with everything else, timber cutting declined during the years following track construction, but for a brief time huge crews worked in the forests along the headwaters of Green and Bear rivers. Whole hillsides were ravaged in the haste to get timber cut, trimmed, and floated down river to the right-of-way, where teamsters freighted the ties to end of track. A few lumber towns managed to survive the collapse by supplying wood for regional needs or shifting emphasis entirely. Hilliard, near the Utah line, produced charcoal through the 1870s for smelters south of Salt Lake and prospered quite well until the smelting industry switched from charcoal to coke.

The dreams of immediate prosperity and a bright future that rolled in and out of rendezvous country on ribbons of steel during 1868 were propped up the same year by the faint glimmer of gold at South Pass. Just the mention of gold, free in the ground for the taking, could move thousands of otherwise sensible and stable men to abandon family, home, and security for a chance to grub in the earth of a distant wilderness; mining was the get-rich-quick-in-the-west syndrome in its apotheosis.

Rumors of a lode near South Pass had persisted since 1842, but it wasn't until a party of Mormons unearthed a small vein in 1867 that the excitement began. By the summer of 1868, more than two thousand men were digging in the gulches and hillsides north of the pass, and three small towns had sprouted at South Pass City, Atlantic City, and Miner's Delight. Stamp mills were hauled in for processing the ore, and there was talk of a rail spur to serve this new Golconda. Despite the enthusiasm, few of the miners were even making wages. A certainty born in zeal (or perhaps desperation) led some to believe that the stamp mill operators were doctoring the assays and skimming off the gold for themselves.

As winter approached, more than half the population departed grumbling, but in the spring the towns filled again with men convinced the mother lode was there waiting for them. Disappointment persisted, though, as the streams stubbornly yielded only enough color to buy food and a few drinks. Miner's Delight was nothing of the sort, and neither were its companion cities; there was none of the spendthrift revelry and rowdy immorality normally associated with mining frontiers, because everyone worked long and hard just for subsistence. By 1873 even die-hard optimists had given up, and the abandoned shacks and stores remained as slowly deteriorating monuments to empty dreams.

Coal lacked the glittering magic of gold, but in time it proved to be a thousandfold more valuable than all the gold dug at South Pass. A subsidiary of the Union Pacific opened mines at Rock Springs and Almy, and by 1880 they were shipping over a half-million tons annually. Though coal may have lacked glamor, it built substantial cities and employed thousands of men. The mining of coal would gradually diminish in the face of cleaner and more efficient petroleum products—diesel oil in locomotives, heating oil in homes and factories—but it pointed out an essential truth of this region: there are no quick and easy ways to success.

In the vanguard of every frontier, just behind those restless scouts who keep to the wilderness because they can't abide civilization in any form, are the incorrigible optimists and dreamers—the promoters, charlatans, and would-be empire builders who chase the mirage of sudden riches wherever unobstructed horizons and virgin lands beckon. But unless the land and the circumstances are particularly ripe, these floaters and drifters move on unchastened to try again, while the real work of carving out a substantial and stable civilization falls to a different breed of people.

The latter are the ones with the clear and simple vision to see the land for what it really is and what it has to offer, and who have the stamina and determination to encourage a reluctant land to yield up a home and livelihood. Such people were the ranchers and farmers who moved into the vast interior of rendezvous country, away from the cindered hopes of the railroad and the mine shafts, to set down roots that still endure today.

Farming has never been an easy proposition in the region, because the potentially arable land is largely arid or semiarid. Except in the mountains and a few favored spots in the northern reaches of the Green River Valley, annual rainfall is less than the fifteen inches generally conceded to be necessary for non-irrigated agriculture; and where rainfall is adequate, the growing season is usually reduced to a mere sixty or seventy days between killing frosts. As early as 1852, Mormon settlers along Blacks Fork recognized the problem and began diverting water to irrigate their crops. From 1860 through 1890 water right entries were made on the Bear, Green, Big Sandy, Hams Fork, and countless other small streams, as individuals, informal groups of neighbors, and land companies built reservoirs and canals to hold the spring runoff and direct it onto their fields. Individual effort in clearing the land and bringing water to it made farming on a limited scale possible. Although the state entered the reclamation business in 1895 under provisions of the Carey Act, followed by the federal government with the Newlands Act of 1902, which created giant projects at Riverton, Fontenelle Dam, and Flaming Gorge, a larger percentage of land in rendezvous country continues to be irrigated by the numerous small projects that began as private responses to a need.

Despite the heroic efforts of farmers, most of the region was better suited to grazing. The grasslands along the apron of the mountains provided ideal cattle country, and in the meadows along the river bottoms wild hay was nurtured and cured by the natural turn of the seasons. Excellent summer grazing was found in the lower mountain meadows, while out in the more arid central portions of the Green River Basin grass was sparser and the stock had to be spread substantially thinner.

Until well into the 1890s the region was open-range cattle country, with stock grazing freely over the public domain; roundups were organized in the spring and fall for gathering, sorting, branding, and shipping the stock. It was a neglected corner of the cattle kingdom, where the open range institutions persisted longer than they did on the plains to the east. Problems of fencing and overgrazing came later

—both circumstances due in large measure to the region's isolation within the mountain barrier. There were protracted battles, legal and physical, between cattlemen and sheepmen, cattlemen and farmers, and cattlemen and cattlemen, but the severe, stock-killing winter of 1898–99 put an end to most of the squabbling. The ranchers, many of whom lost their entire herds, began to exercise more control of their animals as a hedge against another disaster: they began to fence their land and put up hay for the winter, while selective breeding and irrigated pastures become acceptable, even necessary, features of a ranch. It was a less exciting business, but one that made coexistence possible and the future more secure.

There was never to be another era of unrestrained freedom or readily available wealth like that of the fur trade. In its wild places the land might still retain the quality and character of an era when the ground belonged to no man and every live thing took from nature according to its need. But the beaver were gone, the world outside had changed, and the splendid isolation of the mountain man was eroded forever. The men and women who took his place in rendezvous country had seen a different rhythm in the land and felt a different purpose in their bones.

Heirs of the Rendezvous

From the time when John Colter made his first rambling reconnaissance across the northern end of rendezvous country, white men would know the land of the Seedskeedee a scant four decades before the Rocky Mountain beaver trade came to a sudden and uncushioned end. The era of the free trappers and the rendezvous would last less than twenty years, but this brief span established the tone and character for those who would follow. This would forever be rendezvous country.

The beaver men evolved a lifeway that ran in harmony with the land until they became as much a part of the natural scene as any other wild critter. Like the Indians they imitated in so many respects, the mountain men adapted themselves to the land, finding ways to accommodate their needs and desires to the existing framework. They did it because adaptation was necessary to survival—but the suspicion continues that perhaps they loved the land the way it was, and to change it would be to destroy a part of themselves.

Through subsequent frontiers, men who came to mine or farm or ranch found that changing their preconceptions was easier than changing the land—that the path of least resistance was often the most successful. But today we find ourselves in possession of sufficient technical expertise and population to overwhelm the region, to make it over in our own image. While it may be satisfying to realize that man has grown indomitable, to overwhelm this land with the mechanics of civilization would destroy its quality and character—and a proud part of ourselves. Our time, too, has been brief; but it must be a time of caution and caring, lest we snuff out the candle forever.

The heritage remembered: a mountain man at the Pinedale Rendezvous.

Shoshonis and Mountain Crows were frequent guests at rendezvous, and thus their role is a part of the annual reincarnation staged every year at Pinedale, Wyoming.

Another heritage, just as proudly recalled, is preserved on a Blackfoot buffalo robe as the warrior recounts his success in war and the ancient art of horse-stealing.

After a year spent at the edge of survival, rendezvous was a time to relax vigilance and relieve tensions, a time for frivolity and unrestrained joy in just being alive; one might guess that modern life requires the same kind of release.

*Amid ample water and grazing land for their stock, the mountain men gathered six times
close to this site on the* Green River, *near present-day Pinedale.*

Heir to one of the successive frontiers that followed the fur trade in the mountains,
a sheep man rides out to check his flocks in the Wind Rivers.

Once the bane of cattlemen, sheep have since found a place on most stock ranches because they are able to utilize marginal grazing land better than cattle.

Along the foot of the Wasatch Range, in the Weber River Valley, a cattleman pursues his business as experience has taught: open range grazing in the summer, but close herding and feeding when winter clamps down. 137

OVERLEAF: *Colored with the muted hues of a reflected sunset, a working
ranch sprawls beneath the western slopes of* Les Trois Tétons.

Steam clouds in Biscuit Basin. Heat-parched and mineral-poisoned land was one part of "Colter's Hell," which was to become Yellowstone Park.

Part of the Yellowstone "waterworks," Old Faithful has been a consistent magnet for tourists—the latter phenomenon both a blessing and a curse.

141

Latter-day adventurers running the white water of the Snake River
discover joy in the raging torrents that plagued mountain men
and settlers, who would have preferred a placid avenue for commerce.

Mountain water, born clean and pure among the peaks, is a joy and a diversion
for children and visitors—but for those who make the region their home,
it is the vital link to success and survival.

Epilogue:
The New Mountain Man

Against the backdrop of geologic time, man's tenure in rendezvous country has been a flickering instant, no more imposing than a candle to the sun. The Indian came here 20,000 years ago and in his passage left no mark upon the land—except a tradition of leaving no mark. But in the brief 150 years since white trappers first set their traps along its streams and rivers, the region has seen change nearly as startling as the Laramide revolution, which took 40,000,000 years to raise its mountains. Ribbons of steel and stone lie across its face, carrying iron missiles faster than a pronghorn; great holes cut its surface, chasing seams of coal; dams stop the flow of its rivers, and huge lakes stand where none existed before; enduring cities and towns compress more life into less space than the most verdant river valley could hope to do a thousand years before; strange animals graze on its grasses, and fields of crops flourish where wind and clouds had seldom carried enough rain to nourish sagebrush.

Though brief and dramatic by geologic stand-ards, the white man's history was as long in rendezvous country as it was in any other part of the mountain West. The region had seen the whole range of activity common to other frontiers: the years when mountain men trailed the beaver through unspoiled wilderness; the long passing of the overland migration to a more familiar world beyond the mountains; the tumultuous years of the railroad, which brought the pioneers hope for prosperity and a reincarnation of the civilization they had left behind, only to disappoint them with the reality; the irrational excitement of mining; the era of a sprawling cattle kingdom; and the later years of quiet conquest that farms, towns, churches, and schools brought.

Even though the land had known a moving frontier, it was still a young country. Compared to other mountain regions, it was relatively unscarred, and uncongested enough to retain the quality of simple freedom the land had offered to the earliest trappers. Rendezvous country had felt a gentle version of the exploita-

Drink from the waters with reverence, live on the land with caring, and this world will be yours.

tive excess and abuse normally attendant on frontiers, because it offered none of the easy riches. Men who came here worked hard for what they got, so while many came, the land quickly weeded out the weak and the lazy, and the few who remained fit well with the land.

It has never been an easy land to survive in, and it never will be. The weather and isolation exact their toll. But people who have carved out a life here accept the difficulties as part of the price to be paid for living in a world where man and nature are still equal partners. People live here because they want to, not because life is easy; they have found a place and a style of life that fills the need in themselves to experience the world at its most elemental and most beautiful. Whether tradesmen in small towns, or guides and outfitters living at the edge of untrammeled wilderness, they have found a place that suits them, and they have earned it.

The essential quality of this land that drew the mountain men remains for those who seek it, and some men have been seeking it through all the years of development that marked the late nineteenth and early twentieth centuries. What the land offered was freedom: freedom for an individual to make his own kind of life, to build a place for himself with his strength, his instincts, and his determination; freedom from the constant interference of a government of laws, a government too far away to tinker in his day-to-day routine and too far removed in values and priorities to care about protecting him from himself; freedom to measure himself against life at its most basic level.

The people who came to make their homes in rendezvous country were not anarchists or misanthropes—for the most part, they got along fine with their neighbors. They stayed because they found a world in which their actions really had a bearing on the survival and success of themselves and their families. They discovered a way of life where self-deception and parasitic behavior didn't get the job done. There were risks, to be sure—and even tragedy—but the joy of success and accomplishment are greater where risks exist. A person who finally discovers how important he can be to himself finds it hard to give up the life that taught the lesson.

Perhaps the freedom offered by this land is, as some have suggested, only an illusion of freedom; perhaps they are right in contending that from the very beginning the residents have been manipulated and exploited by outsiders. It cannot be denied that the mountain men were victimized by merchants at the rendezvous and put out of business by changing fashions half a world away. Cattlemen and farmers were pawns of eastern-owned railroads and urban regulated markets; almost any enterprise that required any substantial investment ultimately found itself in hock to eastern capital. Certainly there were dependencies that eroded any quintessential freedom, but where life is immediate and fragile, daily concerns assume an importance that overshadows long-term and intangible obligations. If freedom was an illusion, it lasted all day, every day—and that can become a very satisfying reality.

Today more and more Americans seek that freedom, whether illusory or real, in hunting, fishing, back-packing, or pack-training in the high lonesome of the back country. They pursue that phantom called freedom, tasting a lifeway that is a natural by-product of a remote land where institutional progress is held at bay, sampling a world sufficiently challenging to weed out the weak and casually interested.

Rendezvous country is a region at the crossroads. Growing population and an increasingly sophisticated technology could easily overwhelm this island of the past, doing irretrievable damage to the quality of isolation that inheres in the land and eroding the individualistic character of its people with the promises of prosperity and progress that have homogenized so much of this nation. In the long run this land determines the shape of men's lives, and ultimately the earth abides. But over the short haul man will scratch his mark. How deep that mark goes and how beneficial or counterproductive the results will depend largely on how the people view themselves and their land.

The choices ahead are not simple, for there is a tremendous potential for wealth in mining and tourism that presently lies dormant. The Green River geologic formation is blessed with enormous deposits of fossil fuels, principally coal, and other valuable ores and minerals. The rancher who opens his land to development of these resources can expect to become instantly wealthy, and the local economy will benefit from the increased employment that inevitably follows. The benefits are very tangible and welcome, as business booms, the tax base increases, and the kids don't have to go to Salt Lake or Denver to find a job. To men and women who have worked hard all their lives to wring a living from the land, hoping to build a prosperous and secure future for their children, these are real and desirable achievements. It is triumph that can be seen and success that can be measured—two needs not unnatural in the human animal.

But inherent in this kind of development is the risk of results that are just as tangible and not so welcome: crowded cities that breed problems and bureaucracy as fast as they breed jobs and wealth; refineries and processing mills that sully the air with a brown haze; streams once clear and alive with native trout, grown muddy with waste and chemicals; and the sea of grass and sagebrush that was the land's birthright turned upside down. Only the people of rendezvous country can decide how great the risks are and what value is to be placed on the heritage of their land and their lives. To men who have used the game, water, and grass on the surface of this land for more than a century, it may seem only natural to use what lies beneath it as well—but the land grows back more slowly than the grass, and a way of life once lost

could be impossible to recover or to recreate.

The face of this land seems to have as great a potential for generating wealth as the minerals beneath it. People have been coming to rendezvous country to play and to restore their spirits with the tonic of mountain air and virgin wilderness since Capt. William Drummond Stewart of the British Army came out in 1833 to hunt and frolic with the mountain men. Since Stewart's time the land and the institutions have changed somewhat, but the magnetism of the mountains has not diminished, and every year the tide grows stronger as tourists rush to escape the concrete canyons of urban sprawl.

Recreation and tourism seem to be, on the surface, an ideal solution to the region's quandary, for here is an industry that brings baskets of money from the outside world and should take no toll on the land. Tourists come to look at the scenery, and they can never look enough to use it up; hunters and fishermen take a harvest of the wildlife, but never more than can be replaced the following year; skiers may scab up a few mountains, but snow covers most of the damage in winter, and grass grows back in the spring.

The arguments sound plausible, but somehow things haven't seemed to work out that way. Bill Nye, pioneering editor of the Laramie *Boomerang*, wrote in 1880, after a visit to the region, that "on all sides the rusty, neglected and humiliated empty tin can stares at you with its monotonous, dude-like stare." Nye was given only a glimpse of the future, for tourism on a large scale can cut a swath that looks like a battle zone—the impact seeming to grow in geometric proportion to the number of participants involved.

In the private sector, merchants competing for the tourist dollar can sprout a forest of neon and air-conditioning where once a sunlit grove of aspen stood, air conditioned by the prevailing westerlies. Selling the out-of-doors to greenhorns has become a big business, and to make it more attractive, the tendency has been to make it more comfortable. Concrete and steel encroach closer and closer upon the wilderness that is theoretically the attraction, and noisy crowds of motorhomes and motorcycles drown out the quiet serenity—which, screaming billboards have assured the weary traveler, waits just ahead.

It is easy to assume that the problems created by tourism in rendezvous country were spawned by selfish entrepreneurs deliberately and methodically paving over meadows and raising garish tourist snares on the ruins of sylvan glades. If that were true the solution would be simple, for a juggernaut of greed, drunk with profits, careening out of control across an idyllic landscape, makes an easy target. But this is not a situation born of malice; caricatures of feverish rhetoric and simplistic panacea don't fit.

The people who call the region home and make their living by catering to the vacationing campers, fishermen, tourists, backpackers, and hunters know that these visitors are seeking diversions that only uncrowded, unspoiled wilderness can offer. They know that the very presence of large numbers of people and the facilities necessary to meet their needs seriously erodes the quality of the experience they seek. But the flood of visitors continues and grows every year. It might be easy to blame the dude ranchers, guides, and businessmen for the developmental blight that can befall a popular tourist area, but the fact remains that they are only meeting a demand created by countless thousands of people who crowd in to share the experience of this high mountain country.

Of the local businessmen who find their livelihood in tourist dollars, some are dismayed by the growing horde of visitors, despite the fact that more tourists increase their chances of a profitable year. Many of these men and women came to rendezvous country because they loved the land and the life it afforded them; they opened tourist-oriented businesses because it was the only way available to make a living. But the effects of seasonal overpopulation have complicated their lives and partially destroyed the quality of life they came seeking. One crusty outfitter, a veteran of four decades of guiding and dude ranching in the Wind River Range, complained, "It isn't any fun any more; too many folks want it all in a week and a half. I've got people and their garbage all over my mountains—never know when or where I'm going to run into them. They fished all the natives [trout] out of my creek, and now all I got are those damned dead-beat stockers that the Game and Fish boys dump in every year. And the game is scared so bad that I've almost forgot what a bear looks like. There's just too many people for my mountain."

The problems generated by the increasing demands made on the region are faced not only by private individuals, but by the national government as well. The government is the largest landowner in rendezvous country, with federal agencies managing lands acquired as national parks, national monuments, national forests, and reservation lands. The task of determining how to use this land has become increasingly complex over the years in the face of growing numbers of people and an expanding variety of ways to use the finite resources.

Within the realm of tourism the federal agencies must contend with the same kind of overcrowding that plagues the private sector. Providing a suitable and rewarding wilderness or outdoor experience begins to border on the ludicrous when every year more than three million people must be shuttled through particularly scenic areas like the Tetons. Because the needs and desires of these visitors vary so widely, the government must provide—or permit to be provided—everything from luxury lodge accommodations to trails through pristine wilderness. Camping—when space can be reserved far enough ahead to camp at all—has become a nightmare of paved sites and plumbing in canvas-tent and motorhome slums where population density approaches ghetto tenement proportions. Roads are jammed with traffic, and horse or foot trails that loop short of overnight expeditions are alive with the dust of shuffling feet and the gabble of too many voices. Too often excursions to particularly beautiful sites are memorable for all the wrong reasons, simply because too many people tried to dip from the scenic and emotional well at the same time.

This land can still fill the soul and sate the senses with its moods and the shape and texture of the life it maintains. The fulfillment to be found in the wilderness experience is still possible—but it must be sought. The world that Bridger, Fitzpatrick, or Old Bill Williams knew is gone, lost in the growth and change of an inventive, impatient nation, but the essence of the joy and satisfaction those men shared remains a part of the land. It can be found, high and alone where the trappers found it, beyond the point where the easily dismayed and automatically contented have stopped, looked, and turned back. The wilderness and its essence must be reached for, but it still waits here in rendezvous country for those who really want it.

Federal responsibility for lands in the region goes beyond just finding a place to put visitors. Because of its guardianship over national forests, the government must decide how the land and resources of this public trust are to be used. The problems and conflicts are myriad and confusing, and are made more difficult by increasing demands for timber, grazing rights, the region's mineral wealth, water and power development, and recreational land.

The problem is not a new one and does not lend itself to simple and broad-ranging solutions. In 1878, when the federal government was still trying to get all of the public domain into private hands, John Wesley Powell presented his *Report on the Lands of the Arid Region* to Congress. Powell called for an abandonment of the square-grid survey with the 160-acre homestead, advocating a thorough survey of land and resources prior to determining size and disposition of parcels. Land would be divided into units ranging from 80-acre irrigated farms to 2,560-acre stock ranches, with timber and mineral lands set apart in appropriate economic units. The *Report* was the first official recognition that there might be need of some investigation, thought, and planning to realize maximum benefit from the dispensation of western lands. Powell's plan failed to receive recognition and implementation, partly because it would have entailed closing all public land to settlement until the surveys could be completed, and partly because westerners have an ingrained disaffection for having the government tell them how to use their land.

These same stumbling blocks still exist today with modest modification. A demand develops because rising wood prices create a need for more timber, or an energy shortage necessitates more coal, or an extra million tourists want campgrounds with toilets, and the government is pressured into making a hurried decision—which is often determined more by intangible considerations of political expediency than any real evaluation of need and resources. Mistakes can be made—a unique nesting ground is strip-mined out of existence, or a logger clearcuts a slope that starts a process of erosion which wipes out the best part of a sheep rancher's grazing right—and the hollering starts. To the affected public, the government is damned if it doesn't, and damned stupid if it does.

Multiple use has long been the watchword of national forest management, and altogether too many people both inside and outside the government have assumed that the term meant that any piece of ground could—and should—be put to a whole variety of uses. Therein lies the rub that pits timbermen against miners, miners against stockmen, stockmen against sportsmen (the reasons why are almost infinite), and preservationists against everyone.

There are no simple solutions, and there never will be any, but the really distressing aspect is that the problems are growing worse. The resources locked in the forests and mountains of rendezvous country are in increasing demand from a growing population. And those resources are finite, a condition which sadly doesn't seem to extend to our own needs and desires. If the material resources of the region are pillaged carelessly, an incidental casualty may necessarily be that indefinable, almost mystical redemption and restoration that man finds in this wilderness.

In rendezvous country there are critters and varmints. Critters are the useful creatures, and varmints are all the gremlins large and small that can make life miserable. For the mountain man the distinction was easy: critters were the ones that were good to eat, and all the little inoffensive animals that shared the world; varmints, on the other hand, could be the wolverine that ravaged a trap line, the angry grizzly unexpectedly met in the middle of a willow thicket, or the porcupine that ate one's moccasins and hatchet handle during the night. For the ranchers who came along later, the difference was often a little fuzzier, and occasionally even eluded an answer. For instance, the coyote that killed a lamb early in the spring seemed to be a varmint, but then another would spend the rest of the summer clearing out the ground squirrels that were turning the horse pasture into a 470-hole golf course. Things like that made a decision difficult.

There are those who would insist that the meanest, most destructive varmint in rendezvous

Using methods developed over a century ago by men finding their own accommodation to the land, ranchers draw on summer-stacked hay to carry their stock through long and uncompromising winters.

country today is man, and there are times when one might be inclined to agree. This writer's father once stocked a group of high lakes with golden trout, packing for days on horseback with sloshing panniers full of tiny fingerlings. He escorted his delicate cargo with care, dropping them in cold, clear lakes where they could grow and multiply to add another dimension to this mountain world. They were his gift to a land he loves—a land that matched his strong spirit and quiet compassion for the perpetuation of things wild and free.

He returned to those lakes many years later with an animated eight-year-old in tow, who was flush with the excitement of seeing the fruits of his daddy's gesture. It was adventure of a most tantalizing sort, for here was evidence that a man could share a part of himself with the land and leave that portion for his sons and generations of other boys to be shaped into

men in the stern crucible of the wilderness.

There wasn't a golden to be caught that day or any other day. The realization dawned slowly and cruelly, but later investigation finally revealed that some eastern restaurateur, seeking a rare delicacy for his menu, had dynamited the lakes and scooped the once shimmering, full-of-fight bodies from the surface of the concussion-killed waters. To a small boy it was an incomprehensible act, a transgression of values he had grown up to assume were right and therefore the moral law of all men. It was a hell of a way to learn differently. To the father it came as less of a surprise, for he had been on this land a long time, seen the carnage of two-legged varmints before, and felt the smoldering rage that left him dangerously quiet for days.

It took a mindless, worthless varmint to dynamite those lakes, but he was not a rare species. There were many like him who took savagely and destructively from the forests, rivers, and grasslands of this region, without caring or even wondering about the values and spirit that had evolved in this land long before man ever set foot in it.

Man can be a varmint, to be sure; but just as there are different coyotes, there are different men. There will always be the varmints, particularly the human kind who rip their portion from the land and run before Nature can ask its due in return, but they are lessened by their actions— for no man finds an enduring place for himself in rendezvous country until he moves with the rhythms of this land, and shares equally in the cycles of its life.

Modern man is a mover and shaker, thoroughly imbued with a centuries-old habit of making the land over in his own image and armed with the technological muscle to reach his goal. The impulse to rearrange or alter undeveloped land went unchecked and unquestioned for so long that it became almost a conditioned reflex in the American Dream. We have proved time and again that we can redirect the flow of rivers, make barren wastelands bloom, move mountains, and even meddle in the patterns of rainfall.

Rendezvous country is not immune to this libidinal urge in our national character; in fact, in one respect it is particularly susceptible, for it can be—and is being—overwhelmed by sheer numbers of people. To tame and subdue the wilderness may seem the simplest course to many who confront these mountains but who find them too demanding to accept on their own terms. Throughout all the years of our westering, this land demanded that man resurrect his primal instincts, polish his survival skills, and mate both to unquenchable courage and determination if he was to succeed. With our present-day human and mechanical resources, it would be easy to decide that reorganizing the land is preferable to honing ourselves for an encounter that promises less than all success.

But should this land be worn down by our pride in a vision of progress, we run the grave risk of destroying completely the essential quality of the region, and in the process diminishing ourselves irretrievably. Rendezvous country in its native state was the cradle of a legion of American mythic heroes, whose ghosts still tread the high mountain country, evoking the spirit and the values that should remain a cornerstone in our cultural foundation. Their legacy to us lives on in these mountains; to destroy them is to destroy a part of ourselves.

The time of the mountain man is gone, but the place and mood remain for all to savor— just as John Neihardt did in his epic tribute, *A Cycle of the West:*

Who now reads clear the roster of that band?
Alas, Time scribbles with a careless hand
And often pinchbeck doings from that pen
Bite deep, where deeds and dooms of mighty men
Are blotted out beneath a sordid scrawl!

One hundred strong they flocked to Ashley's call
That spring of eighteen hundred twenty-two;
For tales of wealth, out-legending Peru,
Came wind-blown from Missouri's distant springs,

And that old sireny of unknown things
Bewitched them, and they could not linger more.
They heard the song the sea winds sang the shore
When earth was flat, and black ships dared the steep
Where bloomed the purple perils of the deep
In dragon-haunted gardens. They were young. . . .

                   For a little span
Their life-fires flared like torches in the van
Of westward progress, ere the great wind woke
To snuff them. Many vanished like a smoke
The blue air drinks; and e'en of those who burned
Down to the socket, scarce a tithe returned
To share at least the ways of quiet men,
Or see the hearth-reek drifting once again
Across the roofs of old St. Louis town. . . .

Not now of those who, dying, dropped in peace
A brimming cup of years the song shall be:
From Mississippi to the Western Sea,
From Britain's country to the Rio Grande
Their names are written deep across the land
In pass and trail and river, like a rune.

       —From "The Song of Three Friends"

Photographic Notes

The original concept for my color portfolios in *Rendezvous Country* was to relate an awareness, be it only two-dimensional, of a wilderness experience—a photographic orchestration of the wild, untouched land that existed when mountain men first probed into our spiritual heartland 160 years ago. To communicate visually the source of its mystery meant an involved exploration along many trails into the Wind River, Uinta, Beartooth, Absaroka, and Gros Ventre ranges. This I felt would be representative of the pristine wilderness that confronted the trappers and explorers of the 1820s and 1830s.

Today much of the land surrounding the rendezvous sites is pleasant, rolling country speckled profusely with ranches—a settled country. Therefore the mountains had to provide for me the landscape least changed by the encroachment of civilization. For trappers, quest of the beaver pelt was most rewarding in the springtime, when waters were high, weather miserable—and in autumn when snows began to fall. It was my prime desire to relate impressions of the mountains during inhospitable and adverse conditions—a situation these men faced daily. Ferocious storms and walls of rock were also forces that strengthened the concept of opposites. Extreme conditions do exist—untouched, alive, and potent for all to see and feel. At the same time, the delicate detail of windstill reflections or wild flowers in full bloom are realities that invite gentle counterpoints to the harsher landscape.

The mountain man had to survive by his keen instincts. Relying upon instinct helped me to relate on film the fleeting impressions that I experienced. It was most rewarding to find during intuitive wanderings a certain beautiful harmony between man and the primal land. This harmony is elusive and difficult to define or analyze, yet it exists for those who are aware of the natural world around us, wherever it may be. Many of the images I saw went unrecorded by the camera—they were too fleeting to capture—but these basic impressions helped me identify with universal rhythms, the same unchanging rhythms met by the Indians and trappers.

Quietly stalking various animals through forest and meadow and along rocky ledges of alpine heights was especially rewarding. Following bighorn sheep, moose, or elk through the telescopic sights of a 400mm or 560mm lens was intensely exciting—sometimes hypnotizing. I used no special equipment other than a shoulder mount to steady my Leicaflex in open field situations where no tree or rock was available. For close-in work, it was desirable to convey a quiet attitude to animals—patience, a sense of harmony with the scene, and no quick, frightening motions. Holding your whole body system steady can mean the difference between success and failure with animal photography.

I like to travel light, especially on arduous treks into the mountains, so I carry a limited selection of equipment. The more I can forget intricacies of equipment, the more I can concentrate on form and composition of the subject.

Hopefully the camera becomes an extension of my eye. Wherever possible, I used a tripod for steadiness to help express the clarity of mountains, water, and sky.

All photographs were made on either Ektachrome daylight 6115 film (for the 4x5 Linhof Teknika) or Kodachrome II (for the 35mm Leicaflex). Exposures were made from a Weston lightmeter for 4x5 work. Lenses included a 75, 100, 135, 210, 360, and 500mm for the Linhof; a 21, 35, 60, 135, 400, and 560mm for the Leicaflex. Filters—polarizing, 81A, 81B, CC10R, CC10B, CC10G (glass and gelatin)—were used sparingly, primarily to correct a gap in the relationship between what I felt or perceived and what the film actually saw.

—David Muench

Photographic Details

PAGES 2–3: Winter reflections, Teton Range, Wyoming. 210mm Tessar. (4x5)

PAGE 4: Storm aperture of Gannett Peak from Horse Ridge in Glacier Wilderness, Wind River Range, Wyoming. 35mm Summicron. (35mm)

PAGES 6–7: Clearing summer storm over Fremont and Jackson peaks, Island Lake camp, Bridger Wilderness, Wind River Range, Wyoming. 100mm Wide-Field Ektar. (4x5)

PAGES 8–9: Winter dawn on the Tetons above Jackson Hole, Grand Teton National Park, Wyoming. 500mm Tele-Xenar. (4x5)

PAGE 10: Alpine face of Gannett Peak on Wind River Range crest above meandering Dinwoody River. 360mm Apo Ronar. (4x5)

PAGE 11: Autumn mood along Stillwater Fork of the Bear River, Uinta Mountains, Utah; La Motte and Ostler peaks above. 75mm Super Angulon. (4x5)

PAGES 12–13: Temple Peak reflections, Bridger Wilderness, Wind River Range, Wyoming. 135mm Symmar. (4x5)

PAGE 14: Granite Peak north face, Beartooth Range, Montana. 100mm Wide-Field Ektar. (4x5)

PAGE 15: Lower falls, Grand Canyon of the Yellowstone River, Yellowstone National Park, Wyoming. Artist's Point rim. 135mm Symmar. (4x5)

PAGE 16: Fog-shrouded heights above Rock Creek Basin, Beartooth Plateau, Wyoming/Montana. 135mm Symmar. (4x5)

PAGE 33: Frozen interlude in Jackson Hole, Teton Range, Wyoming. 135mm Symmar. (4x5)

PAGE 34: Moose in winter foraging range, Jackson Hole, Wyoming. 400mm Telyt. (35mm)

PAGE 35: Mule deer on slopes of Snake River Canyon below Jackson, Wyoming. 400mm Telyt. (35mm)

PAGES 36–37: Winter sunrise, Gros Ventre River, Grand Teton National Park, Wyoming. 135mm Elmarit-R. (35mm)

PAGE 38: Parry primrose along upper Popo Agie River, Wind River Range, Wyoming. 60mm Macro-Elmarit-R. (35mm)

PAGE 39: Fog-shrouded morning along Crazy Creek, Beartooth Range, Wyoming. 100mm Wide-Field Ektar. (4x5)

PAGE 40: Meandering Yellowstone River in Hayden Valley, Yellowstone Park, Wyoming. 210mm Tessar. (4x5)

PAGE 41: Beaver in home pool along Henrys Fork, West Yellowstone country, Idaho. 400mm Telyt. (35mm)

PAGE 42: Spring outburst of willow catkins along Big Sandy River, Bridger Wilderness, Wyoming. 135mm Elmarit-R. (35mm)

PAGE 43: Moose feeding in willow thicket along the Snake River, Jackson Hole, Wyoming. 400mm Telyt. (35mm)

PAGE 44: White columbine in rock ledge above Seneca Lake, Bridger Wilderness, Wyoming. 60mm Macro-Elmarit-R. (35mm)

PAGE 45: Alpine bloom and fell-field on Beartooth Plateau, Wyoming/Montana. 135mm Symmar. (4x5)

PAGE 46: Lewis Falls and Indian paintbrush, Yellowstone Park, Wyoming. 360mm Apo Ronar. (4x5)

PAGE 47: TOP: Beaver lodge along Green River, Wyoming. 135mm Elmarit-R. (35mm). BOTTOM: Beaver, northern Utah pond. 135mm Elmarit-R. (35mm)

PAGE 48: TOP: Close-up of frog at pool's edge, Uinta mountain country, Utah. 60mm Macro-Elmarit-R. (35mm). BOTTOM: Forest reflections and trout, Big Sandy River, Wind River Range, Wyoming. 135mm Elmarit-R. (35mm)

PAGE 49: Isa Lake reflections along the continental divide in Yellowstone National Park, Wyoming. 135mm Elmarit-R. (35mm)

PAGE 50: Western horned owl, Big Sandy country, Wyoming. Photographed by Bonnie Muench. 55mm Micro-Nikkor. (35mm)

PAGE 51: Reeds and granite in subalpine pool, Arrowhead Peak above Bridger Wilderness, Wyoming. Island Lake trail. 360mm Apo Ronar. (4x5)

PAGE 52: Morning rainstorm, Pingora and Warrior Ridge, Wind River Range, Wyoming. 360mm Apo Ronar. (4x5)

PAGE 53: Tundra garden dominated by blue and white forget-me-nots. Hell Roaring Basin, Beartooth Plateau, Wyoming/Montana. 210 Tessar. (4x5)

PAGE 54: Cirque of Towers, morning reflections. Bridger Wilderness, Wind River Range, Wyoming. 135mm Symmar. (4x5)

PAGE 55: A high-country relict with columbine, along Big Sandy trail, Bridger Wilderness. 100mm Wide-Field Ektar. (4x5)

PAGES 56–57: Rocky Mountain bighorn sheep on flank of Horse Ridge above Dinwoody River canyon, Wind River Range, Wyoming. 400mm Telyt. (35mm)

PAGE 58: Bighorn ram, a close-up face of the wilderness, upper Popo Agie River country, Wind River Range, Wyoming. 400mm Telyt. (35mm)

PAGE 59. TOP: Pika at home above timberline on the Beartooth Plateau, Wyoming. 135mm Elmarit-R. (35mm). BOTTOM: Marmot in granite home on the Beartooth Plateau, Wyoming. 135mm Elmarit-R. (35mm)

PAGE 60: Small herd of buffalo in Lamar Valley range, Yellowstone National Park, Wyoming. 560mm Telyt. (35mm)

PAGE 61: Rydbergia (or alpine sunflower), solo bloom. Photographed by Bonnie Muench in Hell Roaring Basin, Beartooth Plateau. 55mm Micro-Nikkor. (35mm)

PAGE 62: Lone buck in autumn pasture, Popo Agie Wilderness, Wind River Range, Wyoming. 560mm Telyt. (35mm)

PAGE 63: Two bull moose along the Yellowstone River in Hayden Valley, Yellowstone National Park, Wyoming. 560mm Telyt. (35mm)

PAGE 64: Elk foraging along Green River, Wyoming. 135mm Elmarit-R. (35mm)

PAGE 129: Timber Jack Joe from Dubois, Wyoming, in full traditional dress of the mountain man, at the Pinedale Rendezvous, July 1974. 135mm Elmarit-R. (35mm)

PAGE 130: Blackfoot buffalo robe depicting the war exploits of a mountain chief. In collection at the Museum of the Plains and Crafts Center, Browning, Montana. 75mm Super Angulon. (4x5)

PAGE 131: Indian mounts and tepees, Pinedale Rendezvous. 135mm Elmarit-R. (35mm)

PAGES 132–133: Trappers whooping it up, Pinedale Rendezvous. 135mm Elmarit-R. (35mm)

PAGE 134: Old Green River rendezvous sites of 1833, 1835, 1836, 1837, 1839, 1840, Trapper Point, Wyoming. 135mm Symmar. (4x5)

PAGE 135: Lone sheepherder, southwest end of Wind River Range, Wyoming. 135mm Elmarit-R. (35mm)

PAGE 136: Cattle ranch in Weber Valley along the east side of the Wasatch Range, Utah. 500mm Tele-Xenar. (4x5)

PAGE 137: Sheep along Big Sandy River, west side of Wind River Range, Wyoming. 135mm Elmarit-R. (35mm)

PAGES 138–139: *Les Trois Tétons* and farm on Idaho side. 560mm Telyt. (35mm)

PAGES 140–141: Steam columns and pool in Biscuit Basin, Yellowstone National Park, Wyoming. 100mm Wide-Field Ektar. (4x5)

PAGE 141: Old Faithful geyser in evening eruption, Yellowstone National Park, Wyoming. 400mm Telyt. (35mm)

PAGE 142: Running the Snake River below Jackson, Wyoming. 135mm Elmarit-R. (35mm)

PAGE 143: Cascade on a granite stairway along Deep Creek, Bridger Wilderness, Wyoming. 21mm Super Angulon. (35mm)

PAGE 144: My daughter Zandria drinking from a mountain freshet, Cascade Canyon, Grand Teton National Park, Wyoming. 135mm Elmarit-R. (35mm)

156

Index

Body type: American Garamond by Mackenzie & Harris, Inc., San Francisco, California.
Display faces: Murray Hill Bold and Trooper Roman by Paul O. Giesey/Adcrafters, Portland, Oregon.
Printed by Graphic Arts Center, Portland, Oregon.
Bound by Lincoln & Allen Bookbinders, Portland, Oregon.

Design by Dannelle Lazarus Pfeiffer.